The Crisis in Priestly Ministry

OTHER BOOKS BY CHARLES E. CURRAN

CHRISTIAN MORALITY TODAY

A NEW LOOK AT CHRISTIAN MORALITY

CONTEMPORARY PROBLEMS IN MORAL THEOLOGY

CATHOLIC MORAL THEOLOGY IN DIALOGUE

DISSENT IN AND FOR THE CHURCH (Charles E. Curran, Robert E. Hunt, et al.)

THE RESPONSIBILITY OF DISSENT: THE CHURCH AND ACADEMIC FREEDOM (John F. Hunt and Terrence R. Connelly with Charles E. Curran, et al.)

ABSOLUTES IN MORAL THEOLOGY? (editor)

CONTRACEPTION: AUTHORITY AND DISSENT (editor)

The Crisis in Priestly Ministry

Charles E. Curran

FIDES PUBLISHERS, INC.
NOTRE DAME, INDIANA

© Copyright: 1972, Fides Publishers, Inc.
Notre Dame, Indiana 46556

Library of Congress Catalog Card Number: 72-80236
International Standard Book Number: 0-8190-0577-0

To

BILL, CHARLIE, DAVE, JIM,
JOE, PETE, TOM, WALLY;
classmates, students, colleagues
and all those in the priestly ministry
who have been both help and example to me

Contents

Introduction

This book addresses itself to the crisis of priestly ministry. Three aspects are considered—the crisis of identity of the priestly minister, the crisis of spirituality and the crisis of preaching. No attempt is made to develop a theology of the ministerial priesthood as such. Likewise there is no discussion of the question of ministerial ordination and the relationship existing among the various degrees of priestly ministry. The specific scope of reflecting on the crisis of priestly ministry as such also excludes other important considerations such as the question of part time ministry, the ordination of women, a non-celibate priesthood, a temporary priestly ministry.

This introduction tries to describe the context necessary for adequately understanding the limited scope of the book which addresses some theological reflections on the crisis of priestly ministry to those who are either actively engaged in the priestly ministry or preparing for it. In such a limited consideration there lurks the danger of interpreting what is said in a narrowly defined perspective to be the author's complete understanding of the question of ministry. To situate properly the contents of the book itself and to alleviate the possibility of misunderstandings, the introduction will briefly establish the parameters of the book and mention other aspects of the question of ministry which are not developed or touched upon in the following chapters.

This book purposely was not entitled *A Theology of the Crisis of Priestly Ministry*. Too often in the past there has been the tendency to develop theologies of many varied and different topics. The impression was that theology could furnish a thorough understanding of all these different realities. A preferable and more modest approach is to reflect theologically on a particular point. This more limited plan indicates that there are many other considerations, in addition to theological reflection, which are of great importance.

The crisis of priestly ministry obviously involves many different facets of which theology is only one aspect. Theological reflection is most important, but theology cannot solve the problem of the crisis in priestly ministry. Perhaps many people in the Church today are still expecting too much from theology. Since the time of Vatican II and afterwards, theologians have exercised great leadership in the Church. In a sense, the theologian for many people took over the role they often associated with the bishop in the past. The theologian was frequently looked upon as the one who would and should give answers to the problems confronting the Church. Today all should be aware of the important but more modest role of theology and the theologian.

Rather than speak about priesthood, these reflections generally speak about priestly ministry. Sometimes just ministry is used to refer to priestly ministry. This terminology itself indicates important theoretical and practical considerations. The New Testament does not generally use the term priest. In many ways this term owes its origin to other sources. The general tendency today is to make ministry the generic term. Priestly ministry is one form of ministry in the Church. This emphasis on ministry also stresses the serving aspects of priestly ministry. The fact remains that there are many different possible ministries in the Church. Unfortunately, today official ministry in the Church is practically limited to the priestly ministry. Part of the identity crisis comes from the fact that priestly ministry also includes all the other possible forms of ministry in the Church.

These reflections are intended primarily for those involved in, or contemplating entering, priestly ministry today. The first two chapters should also be helpful for all those who in different ways are carrying on a ministry in the Church. The intended audience obviously conditions the tenor and tone of these reflections. The obvious presupposition of these pages is the importance and need of this ministry in the Christian Church. These reflections are offered as a help and encouragement to those involved in priestly ministry today.

However, these reflections in no way should be understood as an argument that it is wrong for someone to leave the priestly ministry. Many different reasons, especially those mentioned in terms of the various crises described in the following pages, could justify such a decision. The Church as such because of its intransigence may be the reason for the decision of some to leave the priestly ministry. I would also be prepared to defend the thesis that priestly ministry of its very nature does not demand permanency so that there can and should be such a thing as nonpermanent priestly ministry. However, the primary purpose of these theological reflections remains to give some insight and encouragement to those who are involved in priestly ministry.

The discussion of celibacy likewise lies beyond the scope of these reflections. There has already been much discussion and writing elsewhere about this subject. This book is concerned primarily with the crisis of ministry as such. To a certain extent such a crisis would still exist even if there were a noncelibate priestly ministry in the Latin rite of the Roman Catholic Church.

However, for some priests today the obligation of celibacy is a very important factor bringing about a crisis of priestly identity. Although a married clergy in addition to a celibate ministry would not be a panacea (as is evident from the experience of Protestant Churches where there is also a crisis of ministerial identity), the law of celibacy is an important reason why many good priestly ministers have left and continue to leave the active ministry. The theological methodology employed in this book, especially in Chapter One, is most favorable to realizing the need for a married, as well as a celibate, priestly ministry. I would strongly argue for

uch a position with the realistic appreciation that
married ministry would be a great help for some
vho are or have been in the priestly ministry even
hough of itself a married ministry will not solve the
risis of ministerial identity today.

These reflections are intended primarily for the
persons involved in or thinking about a life of
priestly ministry. This narrow focus thus cannot
ome to grips with all the aspects of the crisis in
priestly ministry. One could receive a distorted view
f the entire crisis by just viewing it in terms of the
minister himself. This is an aspect which has not re-
eived that much attention thus far in the literature
nd deserves a fuller discussion, but at least in the
ntroduction it is necessary to mention another important facet of the contemporary crisis.

The first chapter refers briefly to the crisis of the
Church itself. Much has been written already about
he problems resulting from authoritarianism in the
Church. At times perhaps there has been an almost
dolescent obsession to blame the Church, its struc-
ures and its officials for all the problems and crises
n the Church. However, the Church and its struc-
ures do have a role to play in trying to come to
grips with the crisis of priestly ministry.

The first chapter points out that from a theologi-
al perspective ministry can and should take a plu-
ality of forms. The crisis arises precisely because
he forms of ministry of the past are no longer
otally adequate today. The individual in his own
reativity must try to respond and build these new
orms of ministry. However, it is impossible for the
ndividual to do this if the Church institution and

its structures do not foster such development. There must be a flexibility in Church structure that helps the individual ministers in the effort to create and develop new forms of ministry, new life styles and new approaches. The need for this flexibility exists in all areas of the Church structure. Dioceses and religious communities must be open to encourage such restructuring. Above all the universal Church must show the same type of flexibility.

The more inductive theological methodology in the matter of ministry as proposed in Chapter One differs radically from the older theological approach which thinks in terms of an eternal and universal priestly essence or nature which then just has to be accidentally modified in different historical, cultural or temporal circumstances. Such an older methodology is still very much present in many official documents of the Catholic Church including the schema on the ministerial priesthood prepared for the Synod of Bishops meeting in Rome in October of 1971. There will and should always be different theological viewpoints within the Church. Likewise theology can never neglect the importance of tradition and its own development, but it can never be tied inflexibly to the past.

In the question of ministry the older theological approaches tend to reinforce the natural institutional bias towards rigidity and unwillingness to change. In any institution there is the problem of inertia, which means that institutional structures as such tend to resist change and remain somewhat inflexible. An older theological method supported such an inflexibility. However, the newer theological approaches call for a much greater flexibility on the part of the institutional Church and its structures. The ministers of the gospel both individually and together must strive for new and more meaningful forms of ministry which obviously will not jettison everything from the past. If the institutional Church does not provide the flexibility for such creative responses, then the crisis of priestly ministry will only be accentuated.

The celibacy question does have importance in itself, but it also has great meaning as a barometer of the willingness to change structure and life styles within the priestly ministry. Continued intransigence in this area by the hierarchical office in the Church will only discourage more and more ministers. The institutional Church must show a greater flexibility if it is to help alleviate the crisis of priestly ministry.

Flexibility in structure will not be a panacea. There will always be the danger that individual ministers will approach the question from a narrowly selfish viewpoint and forget about the wider needs of the people of God either in terms of the needs of a religious community, a diocese or a particular community of the people of God. The collegiality existing among all the ministers of the gospel and their service to the Christian community require that they overcome the temptation of a narrow and somewhat selfish perspective. Obviously there will be some who will react irresponsibly, but this is merely another expression of the Christian understanding of the times in which we live.

This Introduction has touched on other aspects of the question so that the narrow focus of the following reflections will not leave a distorted image. With this background the major thrust of the following pages will consider from a theological perspective the crisis of priestly ministry with the aim of trying to be of assistance to those who are striving to serve God and man as ministers of the Word and Work of Jesus.

This book began as a series of lectures delivered at the conference on "Remaking the Ministry: 1971," sponsored by St. Norbert Abbey and St. Norbert College in DePere, Wisconsin, on the occasion of the 850th anniversary of the founding of the Norbertine order. The creativity and farsightedness exemplified in this form of celebration augur well for the continued vitality of these two communities. I personally am most grateful to the Norbertines for their kind invitation to me on this occasion and for the enlightening discussion and dialogue during the one week in which I participated in their eight week conference.

I.

Crisis in Ministerial Identity

The fact that there exists a crisis in identity among Catholic priests today seems to be admitted by all, but there is a divergence of opinion about the extent of the crisis of identity. The most obvious sign of such a crisis is the number of people who have left the active ministry in the Roman Catholic Church, the diminishing number of those now preparing for the ministry, and the malaise now experienced by many priests.

The aim of this chapter is to reflect on this crisis from the viewpoint of theology. Such a scope remains somewhat limited, for theological reflection obviously considers only one aspect of the question. The multidimensional aspects of the question are illustrated in the study of the priesthood commissioned by the American bishops, which included sections on history, psychology, and sociology as well as theology and scripture. Thus from the very beginning it should be evident that theological resources and reflections are not in themselves sufficient to give a total answer to the crisis of identity in the Christian ministry.

The scope of the present reflections is limited to the crisis of identity in the priestly ministry itself today and does not primarily concern the minister himself or the qualifications and attitudes of the minister. There are many interesting and important points which pertain to such a category—permanency of ministry, celibacy, ordination of women, part time ministry. The theological methodology suggested here will necessarily have great consequences in such considerations, and in my judgment generally calls for rethinking and changing our current practice in these areas. However, to a certain extent these questions remain somewhat less central and important than the more basic and fundamental question of the nature of Christian ministry itself in our contemporary world. In this ecumenical age the experience of other Christian communities reminds us that there is still a crisis of identity in Christian ministry even if the minister is married or female or part time. In the Roman Catholic Church these remain important practical questions, but unfortunately much time and effort seem to be concentrated on these questions when in reality the more fundamental and important question is the meaning and function of Christian ministry in our world.

THE WIDER CONTEXT OF CRISIS

The crisis in priestly ministry cannot be considered apart from the context of our own times, which calls to mind the general characteristic of crisis in much of our contemporary life. Perhaps some would argue that crisis is too strong a word to characterize our present situation and may perhaps overstate the reality. On the other hand there seems to be enough evidence in our contemporary world to justify the crisis situation in contemporary life. The rapid change characterizing our life and culture seems to be an important factor contributing to the many crises of identity in our time. Change makes the older and accepted ways of doing things somewhat suspect. The frequently talked about generation gap manifests on a broad scale the prevalence of crisis in so much of our life today. The fact of such rapid change does not necessarily mean that change is always for the good, for such a simplistic heremeneutic would be totally unacceptable. But in the midst of such great change and among such a plurality of options it is increasingly more difficult to find human meaning.

Bernard Lonergan has maintained that the primary crisis facing theology and Christian life today is not a crisis of faith but a crisis of culture.[1] According to Lonergan there has been a breakdown in the mediation of meaning. The classical mediation of meaning is no longer adequate, but we live amid great multiplicity and complexity with myriad possibilities.[2] The complexity of reality and the many-

[1] Bernard Lonergan, S.J., "Dimensions of Meaning," in *Collection: Papers by Bernard Lonergan, S.J., ed.* F. E. Crowe, S.J. (New York: Herder and Herder, 1967), pp. 252-267.

[2] Bernard Lonergan, S.J., "A Transition from a Classicist World View to Historical Mindedness," in *Law for Liberty: The Role of Law in the Church Today,* ed. James E. Biechler (Baltimore: Helicon, 1967), pp. 126-133.

faceted ways in which contemporary science through its many specializations tries to study and understand reality only heighten the crisis. In the midst of this bewildering complexity and plethora of data the individual person must judge, decide and act. Rapid change prevents a person from merely doing what had been done in the past. The complexity of modern life and science confronts him with myriad possibilities, but the search for true meaning thus becomes only more complicated and difficult. "But judging and deciding are left to the individual, and he finds his plight desperate. There is far too much to be learnt before he could begin to judge. Yet judge he must and decide he must if he is to exist, if he is to be a man."[3]

Lonergan's interpretation and explanation of the general crisis of humanity in our contemporary culture, while not helping at all to positively overcome the crisis, do at least make a positive contribution by indicating and explaining the reasons for the existence of this crisis. Our experience seems to bear out the analysis proposed by Lonergan. Rapid change has at least questioned the past ways of acting. Contemporary man is faced with more possibilities and options today than ever before. There is a tremendous knowledge explosion in all areas of contemporary life, but so much of this knowledge is only data. The search for being human is all the more difficult in this situation. Human meaning is harder to find, and the search requires a person with great maturity and security. The agonizing search

---

[3] *Collection,* p. 266.

for the truly human is evident in the lives of so many people today who are alienated in various ways from the culture and desperately seeking new ways of finding their personal humanity. On a societal level the ever louder call for a reordering of our priorities is merely a reflection of our communal search for human meaning. What does it mean to be human in our society today?

Not only is there a general crisis of the human in our society, but there is also a crisis of institutions. One has only to think of the government and the university to illustrate the lack of confidence frequently existing today concerning institutions. Are our institutions really corresponding to the needs of humanity at the present time or are they so bogged down with the approaches of the past that they cannot really come to grips with the needs and questions of the present? The rapid change of our life and culture seems to be way ahead of our institutions. Likewise the myriad possibilities again actually accentuate the crisis. It is comparatively easy for people today to agree on what is wrong with some existing structures and institutions, but in the midst of many other possibilities it is much harder to find agreement on what should be positively done. All institutions appear at times to be too slow in adapting themselves to the changing needs of the times.

The crisis in institutions today naturally spills over into a crisis of the Church as institution. One cannot consider the crisis of identity in the ministry today without seriously considering the crisis of the institutional Church. Like many other institutions in our society, there is often a credibility gap about the Church. Is the institutional Church really concerned primarily about the gospel it preaches or just about its own institutional preservation?

One of the major problems in the Church influencing the crisis of priestly ministry is the use of authority in the Church. The last decade has witnessed many abuses of authority in the Church and also first attempts to come to grips on a structural level with the abuses of authority. There is great need for a putting into practice the notions of collegiality and coresponsibility. These realities call for important structural changes in the institution of the Roman Catholic Church which are now being discussed but need to be put into practice as soon as possible.[4] There has also been much discussion of a crisis of leadership in the Church which often and rightly blames the bishops for not giving true leadership. However, there do not seem to be many others in the Church, priests or lay people, who are providing great leadership. The stage has passed when one can just sit back and complain about the lack of leadership on the part of the bishops. In many ways there was a euphoric feeling about renewal in the Church during and immediately after

---

[4] In the question of the reform of Church structures, see the studies done under the auspices of the Canon Law Society of America, especially *Who Decides for the Church?*, ed. James A. Coriden (Hartford: Canon Law Society of America, 1971); *The Once and Future Church: A Community of Freedom*, ed. James A. Coriden (New York: Alba House, 1971); *The Case for Freedom; Human Rights in The Church,* ed. James A. Coriden (Washington: Corpus Books, 1969).

the Vatican Council, but the harsh realities of life remind us how slow and difficult a process is required for renewal.[5]

Catholic theology with its incarnational and sacramental principles has stressed the fact that the Church even as institution must be a sign expressing the reality of the Church as the community of those called into existence by the Spirit of the Risen Lord. Too often the institutional Church does not reflect the reality behind it but at times even appears to impede the gospel of Jesus Christ. Does the Church truly operate as the servant of the gospel and the community of the Risen Lord?

Although one must readily admit there exists a true basis for the malaise that many feel about institutions today in general and the Church in particular, there is also present a naive anti-institutional feeling which, perhaps because of an exaggerated individualism, fails to see that institutions and organizations will always be a necessary part of human society. In a true sense man is not free to do his own thing apart from the rest of mankind, but rather men living in community and society will always need organizations and institutions which must constantly be criticized and questioned to insure that they fulfill their proper purpose. Roman Catholic theology to its credit has emphasized that man is by nature a social being and thus destined to live in society with structures

---

[5] For an interesting but very one-sided view on the failure of renewal in the Catholic Church, see James Hitchcock, *The Decline and Fall of Radical Catholicism* (New York: Herder and Herder, 1971).

and institutions. Too often a naively romantic approach wants to do away with institutions or structures. Society and even institutions should not be a restriction of man's freedom but rather furnish an opportunity for him to develop himself and his potential as a member of society and the human community in his life with others.[6]

Likewise in religious circles there has been a tendency to forget the fact that the Church is always a sinful Church which falls short of its function of witnessing to and symbolizing the Risen Lord.[7] In an earlier theology the failure to understand the sinful aspect of the Church resulted in a triumphalism which saw the Church as a perfect society without blemish. Vatican II and the theology brought to the fore at the time of the Council have generally done away with such triumphalism. However, there are many zealous reformers in the Church who have also tended to forget the sinful aspect of the Church because of which it will never totally live up to its exalted goal and function. Once reform did not take place quickly and without difficulty, some in the Church became impatient, disillusioned and disheartened. In any reform movement there is also the danger of forgetting that sin affects the reform movement too. The tendency to forget

---

[6] For an exposition of the traditional Catholic teaching that man is by nature social and the state is a natural society, see Heinrich A. Rommen, *The State in Catholic Thought* (St. Louis: B. Herder, 1945).

[7] Karl Rahner, "The Church of Sinners" and "The Sinful Church in the Decrees of Vatican II," in *Theological Investigations* (Baltimore: Helicon, 1969), VI, 253-294.

he all pervasiveness of human sinfulness can tempt he reformers themselves to become arrogant and even hypocritical.

The sinful aspect of the Church in its own way keeps in tension the human and divine elements which are present in the reality of the Church. On the one hand the Church will never be perfect but as a pilgrim Church will always be tending to be more and more faithful to the Spirit of its risen Lord. To expect the Church to be perfect is an unrealistic demand. On the other hand, the fact that the Church is sinful can never be used as a justification of the imperfections existing in the Church or a rationalization of the actions of many Churchmen. The Christian believes in the continued existence of sin in his own life and in the Church, but he also realizes the call to redemption includes the call to struggle against and overcome the power of sin. The member of the Church thus realizes the imperfections and sinfulness of the Church but also appreciates the vocation to struggle to overcome the reality of sin. Life in the Church will always involve a constant struggle to overcome its sinfulness. Both those who triumphalisticly see no problems with the Church as community or as institution and those who think that the existing problems can be solved easily and quickly fail to appreciate the fact that the Church is always a sinful Church.

An unwillingness to admit any problem with the institutional Church, plus an inadequate reading of the signs of the times, characterizes one part of the document on the ministerial priesthood prepared for the Synod of Bishops held in Rome in the fall of

1971.[8] This document partially describes the crisis of ministerial identity in terms of a secularization in which transcendent realities have no function. "If secularization is understood in this radical way, then faith seems to be excluded and there is no place in this world for priestly ministry, or for the Church itself. The priest . . . loses all meaning."[9]

I disagree first with the analysis of the signs of the times. Yes, there is some of the radical secularization mentioned by the Roman document present in our world today, but there also emerges frequently a great interest in the transcendent and the ultimately religious questions. The signs of the times seem to have shifted in this direction after the over-emphasis on immanence in the 1960's.[10] However, the Church and priestly ministry do not seem to be speaking meaningfully to the contemporary transcendent and religious experience of some people today. We are becoming more and more familiar with the phenomenon of people who are deeply interested in the transcendent and in the need to help others and yet have no interest in or association with the Church. Part of the problem must rest with the Church and its inability to speak to the con-

---

[8] "The Ministerial Priesthood," a working paper for the Synod of Bishops translated and published by the Documentary Service of the United States Catholic Conference, April 29, 1971. For theological reasons I prefer to speak about the priestly ministry and not the ministerial priesthood.

[9] *Ibid.*, p. 2.

[10] As illustrative of this trend in theology, see *New Theology No. 7: The Recovery of Transcendence,* ed. Martin E. Marty and Dean G. Peerman (New York: Macmillan, 1970).

temporary transcendent and religious experience of people in our society.

In addition to the general crisis of culture today and the crisis of the Church, one must also realize there is a crisis of faith. There has been much literature on the crisis of faith, but again some of the underlying reasons for the crisis are those that also are present in the general crisis of culture.[11] The rapid changes in our lives have raised questions not only about the meaning of the human, but also the meaning of the divine. Catholic theology with its generic insistence that the divine and the human are so closely allied that one can know the divine in and through the human should understand the fact that a crisis in the meaning of the human will most readily also entail a crisis in the meaning of the divine. The sociological practices and supports of the faith in an older generation are no longer adequate and are frequently rejected today, but often nothing is found to put in their place. The radical questioning which is characteristic of our age has involved a radical questioning of God and faith. The death of God literature in Protestant theology testifies to this radical questioning and uncertainty.

Often today those interested in reform and change in the Church do not pay sufficient attention to the crisis of faith. For example, many have pointed out the need for new rituals and formats for the sacrament of penance to make it more meaning-

---

[11] Charles R. Meyer, "The Crisis of Faith and Priestly Identity," *Chicago Studies,* VIII (1969), 115-123.

ful and important in the life of Christians. In the last analysis, however, every rite and symbol is nourished in the light of faith and hope. Penance with any format still requires a strong belief in the realities of sin and the merciful forgiveness and redemption of God in Jesus Christ.[12]

CRISIS OF IDENTITY IN PRIESTLY MINISTRY

The crisis of identity in the Christian priestly ministry must be situated in the light of these three other crises—the crisis of contemporary culture and life in general, the crisis of the Church and the crisis of faith. A proper understanding of the crisis of identity in Christian ministry requires a recognition of the general context of crises in which the crisis of identity in the ministry exists. Likewise any attempt to come to grips with overcoming the crisis of identity in the ministry must learn from attempts to overcome these other crises. In general the same factors present in the other crises are also present in the crisis of identity in the ministry—rapidly changing sociological situations in which the older approaches, understandings and structures are no longer totally viable, a radical questioning of existing reality, and a vast complexity making it difficult to find positive meaning and direction.

Specifically, the crisis of identity in the priesthood results from a breakdown and failure of the older understanding and forms to be meaningful in our

---

[12] Carl J. Peter, "Renewal of Penance and the Problem of God," *Theological Studies,* XXX (1969), 489-497.

modern world. Until the last few decades the understanding of priesthood had been heavily influenced by the theology of the Council of Trent and the subsequent juridical understanding of Catholic ecclesiology frequently associated with Robert Bellarmine. Trent understood the priesthood primarily in terms of the power of the priest concerning the Eucharistic sacrifice. Priesthood and Eucharist are intimately connected according to Trent, which thus emphasized the cultic aspect of priesthood and defined priesthood primarily in terms of the power to offer the Eucharist and celebrate the sacraments. In the light of the historical circumstances of the time one can appreciate the reform which Trent brought about even in terms of the pastoral function of the Christian ministry. As time went on, however, especially in the light of the greater juridicization of the understanding of the Church and the priesthood, priesthood was considered primarily and almost exclusively in terms of the twofold power of orders and jurisdiction which the priest had over the physical and the mystical body of Christ.[13]

The theological understanding of priesthood had a great impact upon the self understanding of the priest and his ministry. One can see in this description the roots of many contemporary dissatisfactions. The priest easily became set apart from the laity because he had special powers. In time of distress people would come to him and ask him with

---

[13] James Crichton, "Church and Ministry from the Council of Trent to the First Vatican Council," in *The Christian Priesthood*, ed. Nicholas Lash and Joseph Rhymer (London: Darton, Longman and Todd, 1970), pp. 117-139.

his special powers to intervene on their behalf. Obviously the above description tends to caricature the reality, but such a description is generally accurate.

Vatican II has proposed a different understanding of the Christian ministry by seeing it in terms of the mission and function of the Church itself and describing the ministry primarily in terms of service. Thus the notion of cult no longer remains the exclusive or even the primary way of understanding ministry.[14] Vatican II, however, did not furnish a complete theology of the priestly ministry. The very vagueness and general character of the teaching of the documents of Vatican II perhaps indicate the limits of a theological reflection on the meaning and function of the Christian ministry.

What precisely can theology or should theology contribute to alleviating the crisis of identity in priestly ministry today? One contribution can be in terms of understanding better the crisis itself and the reasons contributing to it. In a sense the first part of this chapter has tried to give such an explanation. Although a better understanding of the crisis and the reasons for it does not furnish a positive approach to overcoming the crisis, it does serve to give an understanding and approach which will help the individual person in coming to grips with the personal problem of ministerial identity. To understand the problem and its dimensions is a first step forward. What more positive contribution can theology make to the crisis of ministerial identity? Theol-

---

[14] Henri Danis, "La théologie du presbyterat de Trente à Vatican II," in *Les Prêtres*, ed. J. Frisque and Y. Congar (Paris: Éditions du Cerf, 1968), pp. 193-232.

ogy can indicate some of the broad lines of the meaning and function of Christian ministry. Theology can criticize both positively and negatively some of the models of ministry which are being developed. However, my main thesis is that theology cannot furnish a total and complete model of Christian ministry for the individual minister to follow in his own life. Theology cannot solve the crisis of identity in the priestly ministry.

One might think that such a thesis is pessimistic and defeatist, for it severely limits the contribution of theology in solving the problem of priestly ministry. However, in the last analysis it puts the responsibility on the shoulders of the individual minister to develop his own understanding and model of Christian ministry. Theology is likewise incapable of solving the other crises mentioned in this paper, although it can make some positive contribution towards such a solution. The sober warning of the underlying thesis of this chapter is not to expect theology to have ready made solutions for such questions as the crisis of ministerial identity. Perhaps in the aftermath of Vatican II theology was given too much credit and too prominent a place in the daily life of the Church. In a sense the theologian replaced the bishop as the important, authoritative figure in the Church who would spell out the proper approaches and thus become the folk hero among the more liberal Catholics. There is still a tendency to expect too many answers from the theologians and the science of theology.

I do not believe that it is a failure of nerve or of responsibility to admit that theology cannot solve

the crisis of identity in ministry or propose a concrete model of what Christian ministry should involve today. Such a thesis should be somewhat lib-
erating for the individual minister of the gospel, for
it places the responsibility on him to creatively develop his own style and model of Christian ministry.
Theological reflection does have something to contribute to the ongoing dialogue on the meaning and
function of ministry especially in terms of generic
descriptions, but it cannot furnish a complete answer or a concrete model to be followed by all ministers. The limitations and the possibilities of theology in this question stem from two major considerations—the nature and method of theology itself and
the nature of ministry itself.

THEOLOGICAL LIMITATIONS

To appreciate the exact nature and also the limits
of theology in general and a theology of ministry in
particular, it might be helpful to consider the limitations of moral theology. Moral theology reflects sys-
tematically on the way in which Christians make
their moral decisions. In the course of studying
moral theology one often raises the question: should
one who studies moral theology be a better living
Christian than the person who does not study moral
theology? One naturally tends to answer this question in the affirmative especially in this day when
we emphasize that one cannot divorce the person
from his work and his function. But a moment's reflection brings about a great hesitation for fear that
one would shunt into second class citizenship all

those who do not study moral theology and the Christian life.

In a true sense this creates a very perplexing dilemma. On the one hand a person's study of the Christian life and the response required of the Christian should have some effect on his life if he is a truly integrated person who does not compartmentalize his life. Yet on the other hand, those who study the Christian life and moral theology do not seem to be better Christians than those who do not study moral theology. My solution to the dilemma indicates the somewhat limited role of moral theology as systematic reflection on the Christian life. I do believe that the study of Christian ethics should have some effect on the life of the person. But other persons in other ways are also able to come to a better understanding and living of the Christian life. Systematic, theological reflection is not the only way to acquire a deeper knowledge, understanding and will to live the Christian life. Christians who are not theologians have many other ways of understanding and living better the Christian life. The study of moral theology is one way, but not the only way or even the most important way of understanding and living better the Christian life. The theologian is not necessarily a better Christian than the nontheologians.

Somewhat the same is true in the questions of ministry. The theologian of ministry is not necessarily a better Christian minister than the nontheologian. The theologian is interested primarily in systematic and reflective knowledge about ministry. The effectiveness of the Christian minister obviously requires much more than knowledge. But even the nontheologian may have a better understanding of Christian ministry than the theologian, but his knowledge is not necessarily the reflective, systematic knowledge of the theologian.

A quick glance over the historical development of Christian ministry indicates that different models and features of ministry have existed at different periods in the life of the Church.[15] The Tridentine model above all emphasized the aspect of cult and defined the priesthood primarily in terms of his power over the Eucharist and the sacraments. This understanding of priesthood is almost entirely lacking in the New Testament; in fact, the New Testament does not use the word priest to refer to the Christian minister.[16] Catholic theology realizes the incompleteness of the biblical message and the need for further growth and development, but the changes between the New Testament time and Trent are quite great. This illustrates very well the various legitimate forms that Christian ministry might take in different historical and cultural settings.

The existing relativity in historical understandings and models of Christian ministry illustrates an important characteristic of contemporary theology.

---

[15] Many of the essays in *The Christian Priesthood* illustrate this historical diversity.

[16] Karl Hermann Schelkle, "Ministry and Minister in the New Testament," *Concilium*, XLIII (1969), 6-19; John A. T. Robinson, "Christianity's 'No' to Priesthood," pp. 3-14, and Robert Murray, S.J., "Christianity's 'Yes' to Priesthood," pp. 16-43, in *The Christian Priesthood*.

Theology today has become much more inductive in its methodology and approach. An historically conscious methodology tries to come to grips with the reality of historical change and development. An older classicist approach to theology proceeded in a more deductive fashion precisely because it paid less attention to the reality of change and development. An older theology thought in terms of universal essences or natures which are true in all circumstances and need only be adapted to the changing historical and cultural circumstances. Thus there was a universal model of priesthood which could then be adapted to the different times and places. However, historical research in the matter of Christian ministry reveals that there has been a much greater discontinuity in the meaning and function of ministry. One must thus adopt a more inductive approach to discover the meaning and concrete models of priestly ministry.

A more inductive approach relies heavily on contemporary experience. Theology thus reflects on reality also in the light of the lived experience of the present so that it cannot construct exact models without the benefit of contemporary experience. Thus theology needs the help and assistance of the empirical and behavioral sciences as well as the practical experience of the life of the Christian ministry. One cannot in an *a priori* and abstract way deduce the concrete model of Christian ministry. There is an interchange and reciprocity between the lived experience and the theological reflection. Theology can and must give general guidelines and directions to the meaning of Christian ministry. Theology must constantly criticize newer models of ministry. However, theology itself is only one factor entering into the dialogue about the precise meaning and function of Christian ministry. A truly historically minded methodology appreciates the need for a greater emphasis on induction without, however, merely passively and uncritically accepting the contemporary experience.

Thus the limitations of theology should be more evident. A more inductive theological methodology needs the lived experience of the Christian ministry. Theology tries to reflect in a rational and systematic way on the meaning of ministry which the Christian minister himself must do in a less systematic and perhaps more intuitive way. These limitations of theology do not open the door for an uncritical acceptance of whatever any minister does as an adequate form of Christian ministry, but they do show the need for the individual minister in the last analysis to develop his own detailed understanding and model of Christian ministry.

A more inductive theological approach realizes the contingent aspects of priestly ministry so that one cannot speak of a universal model of priestly ministry which can serve for all ministers in all circumstances. These are certain generic continuities in the priestly ministry, but these can take many different concrete forms. From the viewpoint of theology, Karl Rahner points out that the concrete form of priestly mission "is open to all kinds of variations from the point of view of ecclesiastical or secular

sociology."[17] Rahner certainly holds for an endur-
ing and continuing element in the priestly office, but
he realizes that "the Church has from the point of
view of dogma an almost unlimited freedom to
shape and distribute its office in such a way that it
really corresponds to its mission and the present
situation."[18]

Perhaps the gravest error in the document, "The
Ministerial Priesthood," prepared for the Synod of
Bishops concerns the theological methodology
which assumes there is a theology of priestly ministry which exists as a universal model apart from the
lived experience of the present and without the
knowledge that the contemporary sciences can furnish about the nature and function of the priestly
ministry. The doctrinal part of the document begins
in a somewhat defensive manner by noting that
many arguments against the ministerial priesthood
come from considerations rooted in human sciences
such as history, sociology, psychology and psychoso-
ciological disciplines. The document somewhat
grudgingly admits that some aspects of ministry are
related to psychological and sociological influences,
but "the reality of priestly ministry was given to the
Church in the mystery of Jesus Christ and arises
from divine revelation, as it is manifested in the
Bible as understood in the Church's tradition."[19]

---

[17] Karl Rahner, S.J., "What is the Theological Starting Point
for a Definition of the Priestly Ministry?" *Concilium,* XLIII
(1969), 86.
   [18]*Ibid.*
   [19] "The Ministerial Priesthood," p. 5.

"We know the nature of Christian priestly ministry only through divine revelation which offers us the fundamental teachings above the eschatological service of Christ and the Apostles."[20]

The methodology of the document prepared for the Synod of Bishops rightly stresses the importance of the Scriptures and tradition, but gives the impression that Scripture and tradition furnish a concrete model for priestly ministry today. There are important and fundamental aspects of ministry found in the Scriptures but these remain very general and capable of very diverse historical manifestations. This document is based on a theological methodology that has been abandoned by most Catholic theologians today. This methodological error lies at the roots of the false conservatism of this document and prevents it from really coming to grips with the question of concrete models for Christian ministry today and the qualifications and dispositions required of the Christian minister today.

Thus the more inductive nature of theology and of its systematic reflection on the Christian ministry prevents theology from proposing any concrete models of priesthood which are viable for all ministers, in all different historical situations. A more inductive approach will be able to propose only tentative models and will greatly depend upon the contemporary experience of those who are trying to live the life of the Christian minister in our contemporary society. This more inductive and somewhat empirical approach will also call for dialogue

---

[20] *Ibid.*

with the behavioral sciences. There is no such thing as the universal or eternal model of ministry which can serve as a concrete model for Christian ministers.

MANY POSSIBLE MODELS
OF PRIESTLY MINISTRY

The nature of Christian ministry itself also affords a myriad of possible models of ministry. Since ministry in some way involves ministering the Word and Work of Jesus to mankind, it is impossible to describe it in terms of a very concrete and tight model. The very complexity of the human and the different possibilities which underlie much of the contemporary crisis of culture also lie at the heart of the crisis of ministry. The human being today in the midst of a bewildering complexity must choose for himself what seems to be the truly human. Likewise the Christian minister is faced with a staggering complexity in his search for a model of ministry. In this way Christian ministry precisely because it has to do with the human is not able to have the strict definitions and boundaries which other professions and vocations might have. Christian ministry thus shares in the crisis of the human at the present time because by its very nature it can be as broad as the human. Being human today is something different from being a sociologist or a doctor or a computer programmer. All of these jobs or professions are somewhat well defined. Being human requires a broad knowledge of many things, but the very breadth of the human does not allow for deep specialization in any one field. Today there is an increasing move towards specialization because of the greatly increasing complexity, but this only heightens the tensions of trying to be human. However, we also react against the specialists who run things from their own narrow perspectives and fail to see the wider human implications. It is very difficult to define the competence of the human just because it ultimately must embrace so much and cannot afford the luxury of specialization in a particular area. Trying to be human can be a difficult and frustrating attempt today, but it is more necessary than ever before.

In many ways the ministerial priesthood as the servant of the Word and Work of Jesus shares in the crisis of the human. The ministry is directed to all men and thus takes on a universality because of those it wishes to serve. The ministry is directed to young and old, black, brown and white, city dwellers and farmers, workers and business men, professional people and the handicapped. Likewise there is a universality about the message of Jesus which is relevant for the daily life of all these people. One who tries to minister the Word and Work of Jesus thus will often feel pulled apart by the universality of the demands made upon him. By being stretched so broadly he is not able to have the security of specialization and concentration on a particular area. Since ministry is so related to the human in all its dimensions it is bound to share in the same crisis of identity.

The New Testament reminds us that there was a great plurality of ministry even in the early Church. Paul mentions apostles, prophets, evangeists, pastors and teachers (Eph 4:11). Unfortunately the historical development tended to reduce all forms of ministry in the Church to priestly ministry. The very fact that ministry can and has taken many different forms indicates again the plurality of ways in which the ministry can function. The fact that priestly ministry lately has tended to become the only official ministry in the Church for all practical purposes has only heightened the tensions.[21] Obviously there is need to recognize the multiple forms of ministry and the fact that different people should and could fulfill these functions. However, this will still not solve the problem of the exact model for priestly ministry.

The general thesis of this chapter is that theology cannot offer a concrete model for priestly ministry which every minister can then adopt. Ultimately the individual minister himself must responsibly fashion his own ministerial role in terms of the people he is trying to serve and the circumstances in which he finds himself. The Word and Work of Jesus can take on innumerable forms. Theology can and should provide broad guidelines and offer criticisms, but ultimately the concrete meaning of ministry comes from the individual minister himself. The limits of theology in this matter only underline the important responsibility of the individual priestly minister to shape his own ministry.

Edward Schillebeeckx has proposed the same basic thesis in somewhat different terms. Schille-

---

[21] This fact is frequently referred to in contemporary theological writing on ministry, as is evident in the synopses of recent research on the Christian ministry prepared in file form by *Prospective*, Avenue Armand Huysmans 77, 1050 Brussels, Belgium.

beeckx schematically defines the priesthood in
terms of three fundamental ideas: the priest is the
servant of the Word, he preaches and presides at the
sacramental life of the Church, and he is the leader
and animator of the ecclesial community in the
name of Christ. These fundamental concepts, however, require an explanation. These ideas express
the complete content of priestly ministry without
specifying the concrete forms of expression and
realization of priestly ministry. The concrete and
specific question can only be answered in the light
of the situation of the present.[22]

ILLUSTRATION OF THE THESIS

To illustrate the general thesis of this chapter
some of the newer approaches to the meaning of
Christian priestly ministry will be considered. In
general, contemporary Catholic theology tends to
describe priestly ministry primarily in terms of leadership and service in the Christian community. The
more specific aspects of the priestly ministry include
the celebration of the Eucharist and the sacraments,
the ministry of the Word, the organization and leadership of the Christian community, and the incarnation of the Word in justice and love.[23] A consid-

---

[22] E. Schillebeeckx, "Theologische kanttekeningen bij de
huidige priestercrisis," *Tijdschrift voor Theologie,* VIII (1968),
402-434.

[23] For the best bibliography on the question of priestly ministry, see *Bibliographie internationale sur le sacerdoce et le
ministère,* 1969, ed. André Guitard and Marie-Georges Bulteau
(Montreal: Centre de Documentation et de Recherche, 1971).
Earlier bibliographies were published by them in a slightly different format.

eration of the general notions of leadership and service illustrates the problematic mentioned above; namely, the terms are so broad that they can include a great variety of ways of implementation.

There are many people who should and do exercise leadership in a community. One does not have a monopoly on the talents of leadership. Likewise there are many ways of serving the Christian community and many people who are actually involved in the function of serving the Christian community. At best this description gives some broad outlines to the understanding of ministry, but it still leaves the individual minister with the responsibility of discovering what service and leadership mean in the specific ways of exercising his own ministry within his community. Although such directions are helpful they cannot of themselves overcome the crisis of ministry which in the last analysis can be solved only by the creativity of the individual minister himself.

Even the more specific descriptions of Christian ministry do not furnish a solution to the crisis of ministry, for they again must leave much room to the creative and integrating responsibility of the individual minister. Perhaps the most easily definable and explainable role of the priestly ministry is the cultic function of ministering and celebrating the Eucharist and the sacraments. Since such a description is somewhat narrow and specific there is less complexity and ambiguity than in the other more general descriptions of Christian ministry. Here there is a greater opportunity to develop a more specific and concrete description of this aspect of priestly ministry. However this remains only one aspect of the ministry, and even here problems of identity exist and are heightened by the change from the Tridentine understanding.

The older concept of the power to consecrate and offer the sacrifice of the Eucharist obviously stressed the *ex opere operato* aspect of the sacraments. These sacramental acts produced grace for all who would come into contact with them and have the necessary dispositions. Today there is a recognition that the sacraments and even the Eucharist are not primarily channels of grace or even the only way in which one comes into contact with the love, mercy and forgiveness of God in Jesus Christ. The whole life of man is sacramental and brings man into contact with the God of redemption and salvation. The sacramental celebrations are precisely intensifications and celebrations of the reality of God's saving presence in our midst. The Eucharist and the eucharistic community must then be seen in some relation to the daily life of the community. In the Eucharist the community celebrates its faith in the Risen Lord which it then tries to live in its life. The eucharistic community by its very nature must be more than just a group of people who come together for the Eucharist on Sunday morning. The priest must also be a part of the daily life of the community so that he can properly celebrate its faith in the Euchrist.

This changed understanding of the Eucharist is obviously the ideal, but we all realize that practice will often fall far short of that ideal. Yet there is a realization that the present structures and practice must somehow or other be more in keeping with the ideal of the meaning of the eucharistic celebration by the community. But problems exist on all sides. There is the problem of the large number of people who really do not form a true community. There is the fact that in our contemporary society with its plurality that people generally live in many different communities so that there is little hope in expecting the eucharistic community to continue a truly community existence throughout the daily life of its members. Many Christians will always be satisfied with a minimum of participation, but the Church, as distinguished from a sect, must be willing to minister to and to serve all God's people even if their Christian commitment is not that explicitly primary in their daily life.

Obviously present structures such as parishes and dioceses tend to correspond to the older understanding of ministry, and there remains great difficulty in trying to form newer structures more in keeping with our contemporary understanding. The priestly minister must know that he will never have the perfect eucharistic community and very often must be content with imperfect images and flashes of what such a community should truly be. Yet the minister is called upon to creatively find ways and structures in which the eucharistic community and its celebration can be understood in terms of the daily life of all concerned.

The sacrament of the anointing of the sick well illustrates the malaise experienced by many priestly ministers in the cultic aspect of their ministry. The basic idea of the sacrament is most appropriate. The saving Word and Work of Jesus should be visibly present to Christians at important moments in their lives. Grave sickness certainly is one time in which it is proper and fitting to celebrate the saving power of the Risen Lord with regard to the sick person. The sacramental rite is above all a faith celebration in which the faith response of the person is joined with the prayer of the priest, family and friends.

How different is the reality! In a hospital emergency room the doctors are frantically working over the patient trying to revive him. They allow the priest to enter and quickly anoint the dying person with the short form. The grieving relatives are ever so happy that their loved one had the last rites of the Church. The minister somewhat frustrated and irritated by the magical character of the whole process mumbles a few pleasantries and then leaves. Obviously a renewed education concerning the whole meaning of the sacraments is called for; then there is need to adopt structures and practices to this better understanding. But these involve time and patience before they can be brought about.

The role of the minister in worship today calls for a much greater faith participation on his part. In a one-sided *ex opere operato* approach the faith participation of the minister was deemphasized. The sacraments had their effect of producing grace independently of the disposition of the minister. There is a valuable theological truth in such a statement, but at best it represents the very minimum acceptable for a sacramental celebration and in no way corresponds to what the reality should be. Today we realize the sacraments are signs of faith, and the minister especially celebrates them as a man of faith. The personal faith of the minister should be an important part of the sacramental celebration. The spontaneous prayers which are more frequently (and rightly) becoming part of sacramental and eucharistic celebrations underscore the personal faith involvement of the minister. There are some priests leaving the active ministry today because of problems of faith. Now more than before, the faith of the minister must be more present in the eucharistic and sacramental celebrations.

The cultic aspect of priestly mininstry does remain quite well defined, but this is only a part of the total ministry. Here too, however, the older understandings and structures are no longer adequate for our contemporary understandings. There is an urgent need for education and new structures, but there is very little agreement on concrete steps to bring this about. The priestly minister lives in the tension of realizing how the present falls far short of the ideal and patiently tries to work for change and renewal.

The second specific theological description of Christian ministry is the ministry of the Word. The Word of God as a living Word embodying the good news has meaning and relevance for the life of God's people The ministry of the Word strives to mediate this living Word to men in all the varied facets of their existence. The general cultural problem of complexity enters here because the Word of God must be addressed to men in all the situations of their lives. A separate chapter will discuss the particular question of how specific the preacher of the Word should be on particular questions and issues.

The ministry of the Word raises other problems and questions. The minister must obviously be acquainted with the Word of God and theology. However, it may be true that there are other people in the community who have a better knowledge of Scripture and theology. The average minister of the Word realizes his own theological shortcomings and does not always have the opportunity or the time to develop his theological knowledge. To preach the Word thus seems to call for a great knowledge of Scripture, theology and the concrete situation in which people find themselves. Here again the minister finds himself somewhat frustrated by the complexity of the situation and the many demands made upon him which appear to place on him burdens which he cannot fulfill.

The role of the minister concerning the Word of God is not the only teaching function within the Christian community. As a matter of fact the teaching function in the Christian community is most often carried out by those who are not ordained ministers. What is the exact relationship between these different types of ministries in the Church? There is also another important aspect of the ministry of the Word which is not necessarily connected with the office of ordained ministry. This is the prophetic function of preaching the Word. The prophetic function is not always identified with the priestly ministry and most often in history has been found outside the priestly ministry. Thus again there are multiple ministries of the Word of God which are not necessarily identified with the priestly ministry.

The fact that the Word of God should be mediated to men in their daily lives lies behind the theological understanding of the sacramental system. The sacramental system realizes that the Word and Work of Jesus should be present to man in the more important times of his life in such a way that the whole life of man is thus seen to be sacramental. By celebrating at important moments the sacramental liturgy tries to indicate that the whole life of man is sacramental. One way to understand the sacramental system is in terms of important moments in the lives of people—birth, times of nourishment, sickness, etc. This sacramental system thus in miniature reflects the attempts to mediate the Word of God to men in their daily lives. However, life is infinitely more complex today. There are many important situations today to which the Word of God should be addressed, but the minister can not hope to have the requisite familiarity with all these things. Thus the minister is left with the difficult task of deciding how and when, since he cannot possibly expect to mediate the Word and Work of God to man in all the situations of man's life.

Another more precise and specific description of priestly ministry is in terms of the organization and leadership of the Christian community. There is no doubt about the fact that at the Eucharist or the community celebration the priest is presiding. This indicates his organizational and leadership role in the life of the community. However, many problems emerge in considering this role. Individual Christians belong to many different communities besides their Christian community. One cannot expect or perhaps even desire that the Christian community be the only community in the lives of people. Even within this one community there is need for a multiplicity of talents and ministries.

An older understanding of societal life saw everything as structured from the top down with leadership being some form of power conferred by office. Since the priest was the ordained minister for the community, he obviously was the leader of the community. Today there is a growing realization that leadership does not depend on office but often is a function of the talents and abilities which various people have. Just as there are a plurality of ministries in the community so too there are a plurality of talents. The priestly minister can serve as a leader in trying to bring all these people together for the good of the total community. To talk about leadership in the area of liturgy is easy, but to talk about leadership in other areas is much more complex. Generally it will be impossible to describe the exact nature of this leadership, for much will depend upon the talents of the individual minister and the talents and needs of the particular community.

Another problem comes from the fact that so much emphasis today is rightly placed on coresponsibility in all aspects of the life of the Christian community. The priest should not be a leader in the sense of completely dictating to the community. Even in the living of the Christian life, while the minister should strive to be as perfect a witness to the gospel as possible, there will always be others in the Christian community who can and should be leaders in terms of the response to the good news.

The functional role of the leadership of the minister then will vary and depend quite heavily on contingent circumstances. Again the responsibility devolves on the minister himself to see how his leadership should be exercised in the Christian community.

Another specific description of the role of the priestly minister is in the area of the incarnation of the Christian message of love and justice. There can be no doubt that in the past the mission of the Church, which was usually synonymous with the mission of the priest, tended to be too individualistic. The pastoral ministry was primarily directed to the care of the individuals. Certainly this will always remain an important aspect of the mission and function of the Church and her priestly ministry. In this area too the priestly ministry should not only be in terms of consolation and solace but also in terms of urging people to a greater participation in the working for justice and charity. But it will never be enough merely to urge individuals to work for peace, justice and charity.

The mission of the Church and to some extent the mission of the priestly minister must also be in terms of societal structures. This fact is becoming more evident in contemporary life. The Christian message exists not only for individuals but also for society as a whole. Efforts must be made to change society so that it makes justice, peace and charity more possible and feasible for all.

Here too the problem of complexity and knowledge enters in. It is not enough merely to talk in general about love, justice and peace. Christians are facing concrete problems of great magnitude in areas of justice and peace. Leadership from a Christian perspective in these areas requires something more than just general utterances. But again the problem of complexity arises. There are many such problems. Each problem is very complex in itself and requires a great deal of knowledge and sophistication. The danger of the "do gooder" who brings much enthusiasm but little practical knowledge and help is ever present. The minister is obviously faced with this staggering complexity and has difficulty in knowing precisely what should be done.

In the area of justice and peace the Christian mission has to be more than just talk and words. The priestly minister must strive to find ways in which the Church and he himself can contribute to the actions needed in society. However, there are many great limitations on the function of the Church and the minister in this area. The work of changing society and making it more just is not the primary function of the Church or the minister. There are many other persons and groups who are involved in this work. Events in some movements for social justice in the last decade remind us that the role of the Church is not that of the leader, for too often this amounts to a type of paternalism. Often perhaps the Church and the priestly minister can act in some way as enablers for others.

The more specific descriptions of priestly ministry while serving as guidelines really do not solve the crisis of identity for the priestly minister. Another frequently espoused description understands priestly ministry as the symbolic center of unity in the community. But such a description by its very nature creates its own tensions and problems. It is true that the priestly minister in a sense is and should be the symbol of unity in the community, but every community needs both unity and diversity. Too often in the past uniformity has been substituted for unity. Likewise it is necessary at times for the minister to be prophetic and a sign of contradiction within the community. In many ways, especially in the short run, these functions do not enhance the unity of the community.

In the midst of discussions about priestly identity there frequently arises discussion about professionalism in the priestly ministry. Obviously an age such as our own appreciates and prizes professionalism in work. Priestly ministry should be exercised in the most professional way possible. However, I personally cannot agree with some of the trends I see taking place in the name of professionalism. The underlying theme of this chapter is that the crisis of identity in ministry comes ultimately from the fact that there is a universality about ministry much the same as there is about the human. One false attempt to solve the tension comes from collapsing priestly ministerial identity into some other form of professional identity. Priestly ministers take too easy a way out if ultimately they try to solve the crisis of ministerial identity by finding their identity primarily as social workers, teachers, counselors or community organizers. If one sees his whole identity in these other professional terms then he loses some of that universal humanism which is part and parcel of priestly ministry.

Mediating the Word and Work of Jesus to man does in a sense make a person a generalist and submits him to the tensions of one who feels that he is jack of all trades and a master of none. But ministry does seem to call for such a generalist orientation. The generalist always suffers from the realization that he cannot indulge in specialization in any particular areas. However, in our contemporary society we have begun to realize the evils of too great a specialization so that the general, human viewpoint is not expressed. Society today is reacting against letting the technocrats run the society or the military run the defense department. Too often the narrow specialist sees things only through the limited horizon of his own specialization and fails to take the truly human vision. It is much harder and difficult to define and know what the truly human horizon is, since by its very nature it is much broader and more inclusive than the horizon of a particular specialization. But this is what brings about the contemporary crisis of culture and likewise the crisis of identity of the priestly ministry.

The generalist nature of priestly ministry does not argue against some forms of specialization. The very fact that this ministry can take on many different forms means that each minister must somehow or other specialize in certain areas and aspects of the priestly ministry. My objection is to finding the identity of the minister in terms of another profession or specialization rather than seeing the ministry as taking on many possible forms.

CONCLUSION

This chapter has consisted of theological reflections on the crisis of identity in the priestly ministry.

Part of the function of a theological reflection is to identify and try to understand the reasons for such a crisis of identity. The crisis of identity in priestly ministry must be seen in the context of the times, which includes the crisis of the human in our culture, the crisis of faith and the crisis of the Church. Specifically there is a crisis of identity in the priestly ministry because the older life format and structures no longer correspond to our newer understanding of the meaning and function of the ministry.

However, theology alone can never take the positive step of developing a concrete model for priestly ministry which all priests can then follow. This stems from the very nature of a more inductive theology and from the nature of priestly ministry. Priestly ministry involves the service of the Word and Work of Jesus and the Christian community. Where the Word and Work of Jesus as well as the Christian community are most explicitly and intensely present is in the sacramental celebrations especially the Eucharist. Here the role and function of the minister are quite clear.

But the Word and Work of Jesus as ministered to the Christian community take on many different forms, precisely because the Word and Work of Jesus should be meaningful to people in all the aspects of their lives and should have something to contribute to all aspects of truly human life. The Word and Work of Jesus as lived is just as broad as the reality of the human. Thus ministry has about it a generalist character much like the generalist character of being human in our complex life and world. Ministry thus can and should take on many different forms and approaches. The ministry of the individual priest will greatly depend on his own talents and the needs of the community and the people he serves.

It is the generalist nature of Christian priestly ministry which argues for the fact that theology can never produce a concrete model of ministry which can serve adequately for all ministers. To think that theology can solve the crisis of identity in priestly ministry is a false hope that should be rightly shattered. The crisis in identity arises from the generalist character of priestly ministry and the resultant fact that ministry can and should take many different forms. The crisis is more discernible today because the older formats and understandings of priestly ministry no longer seem viable. But in the midst of bewildering complexity it is difficult to find models and formats for Christian ministry. Theology alone will never be able to present such concrete models. The primary responsibility rests with the priestly minister himself.

The priest must be a person who is deeply committed to ministering the Word and Work of Jesus to the Christian people and the Christian community. He must be creative enough to find the best ways for carrying out this ministry in the midst of myriad possibilities. The frustration and anxiety of the minister today often come from his own insecurity and inability to find meaningful ways of ministering to God's people. He must be constantly willing to experiment and try new methods and approaches. Many times these approaches will not be successful, but trial and error is a very important part in the learning process of finding out the meaning of Christian ministry in the complex circumstances of modern life. The creativity of the individual priestly minister will be helped by a constant dialogue with other priestly ministers and also with theologians, sociologists, psychologists and others who can assist him in trying to discover the forms of priestly ministry most appropriate and effective today.

Adding to the tension is the fact that the Christian ministry will always reflect the basic eschatological tension present in the Christian life. As Christians and as priestly ministers we all fall short of the eschatological perfection to which we are called. We live with the imperfections and frustrations of the present in the hope of the future. The priestly minister will never find the perfect form of ministry but must always try to develop better ways of ministering the Word and Work of Jesus to men.

The crisis of identity is part and parcel of the very nature of priestly ministry and is the challenge which accompanies such ministry. This is even heightened today by the breakdown of the older structures and the failure of the older forms. Perhaps for the first time we are beginning to realize the great plurality of forms which Christian ministry can and should take. The individual priest must discover for himself how he can best accomplish his ministry. This requires that the priest be a person committed to the service of the Word and Work of Jesus and of the Christian people. Too often in the past and perhaps even in the present the priestly

minister expects others to solve the crisis of ministerial identity. Obviously there are very important
foundational realities that are common to all forms
of priestly ministry. However the crisis of identity
as described here comes from the concrete ways in
which the priest should carry out his ministry. This
is the challenge which only the individual priestly
minister himself can solve in collaboration with
other ministers and with those in the Christian community such as theologians, psychologists and
others who can be of assistance in this quest.

II.

Crisis in Spirituality

The existence of a crisis of spirituality in priestly ministry needs no long documentation or proof. In many ways this follows naturally from the crisis of identity existing in the priestly ministry. Many of the same factors underlying the crisis in identity in priestly ministry and the other crises of our contemporary culture are also present in the question of priestly spirituality.

THE SIGNS OF THE TIMES

The accepted forms of the past are no longer meaningful and operative today. In many ways the spirituality of the priest in the past was based on the monastic model, but the vast majority of priests are not monks.[1] Less than ten years ago the one aspect

---

[1] For early attempts to develop a spirituality for diocesan priests which recognized at least some difference from the monastic model, see Eugene Masure, *Parish Priest* (Notre Dame, Ind.: Fides, Publishers, 1955); Gustave Thils, *The Diocesan Priest* (Notre Dame, Ind.: Fides Publishers, 1964).

of priestly spirituality which was acknowledged by almost all priests was the breviary. In addition a good number of priests faithfully prayed the rosary. Most realized the need for some meditation, but the majority did not seem to follow the regular practice of morning meditation which had been the regimen of their seminary life. Spiritual reading was sporadic.

In the early 1960's a few priests began to pray the breviary in English because they realized the breviary was supposed to be a form of prayer, but Latin was more of a hindrance than a help to prayer. Finally through the liturgical changes associated with Vatican II the breviary was put into the vernacular. At first many priests appreciated the advantage of praying the breviary in English and made some effort to pray the breviary and not merely recite it. However, within a very few years the breviary did not seem to be a meaningful prayer form for a good number of priests. Today many priests do not pray the breviary daily.

One of the reasons behind this dramatic switch in the prayer life of priests was a better understanding of the breviary obligation. Moral theology rightly began to question those obligations which in the popular mind existed under penalty of mortal sin. Mortal sin is not a pain or a penalty. Mortal sin is the reality of man's breaking his relationship of loving dependence upon God. Mortal sin is obviously an important and comparatively rare event in the life of the Christian. Mortal sin consists not in the matter or the thing itself but rather in the breaking of this fundamental relationship which

inds the Christian in love to God, neighbor and the
world.[2]

Since the matter of the breviary in itself cannot
constitute such grave matter and since mortal sin
cannot be viewed primarily in terms of the matter
or thing itself, many priests began to realize that
there could be no such grave obligation attached to
the daily praying of the office. The suspicion arose
that the gravity of the obligation was created by the
Church to make sure that priests did recite the breviary. Such obligational thinking is no longer conso-
nant with the theology accepted by many priests
today. Many younger priests did not even have to
struggle with the decision not to pray the breviary.

Another factor for some priests was that the breviary no longer seemed an apt form of prayer for the
priest today. They experimented with other forms
of prayer and often substituted something, such as
reading of the Scriptures, in place of the breviary.
Many priests discontinued the divine office, but did
not substitute anything in its place. Other forms of
prayer such as the rosary had long since been aban-

---

[2] John Giles Milhaven, *Toward a New Catholic Morality*
Garden City, New York: Doubleday, 1970), pp. 85-97; Kevin F.
O'Shea, "The Reality of Sin: A Theological and Pastoral Cri-
que," *Theological Studies,* XXIX (1968), 241-259. Even from
canonical perspective it seems that the praying of the breviary
or those in major orders is only a light obligation. See, Martin
emple, "The Divine Office: How Serious An Obligation?"
Homiletic and Pastoral Review, LXIX (1968-69), 596-603. This
rticle is based on an unpublished doctoral dissertation written
by Semple in the School of Canon Law of the Catholic Univer-
ity of America, "The Obligation of the Divine Office in the Latin
nd the Oriental Churches."

doned by many younger priests. Obviously there was a developing crisis of prayer. An intelligent celebration of the Eucharist did call for some preparation especially in terms of a homily so that in this way priests did have some true prayer life, but there was an uneasy feeling that a stronger and deeper prayer life was needed.

Obviously the crisis of prayer also exists outside the priestly ministry. Perhaps part of it is due to an over-reaction in our whole thinking about God and man. The theological shift in the 1960's from transcendence to immanence placed more emphasis on man and less on God. Man now assumed responsibility to bring about the new heaven and the new earth. The death of God and some currents of the secular theology movement overemphasized the role of man and forgot the divine.[3] However, there is now a changing emphasis in theology as in many areas of contemporary life on the importance of transcendence. This movement is now searching for better forms and types of prayer. One interesting sign of this fact is the number of houses of prayer which religious communities and diocesan priests are establishing throughout the country. Priests, like many others today, are searching for a prayer life and for forms of prayer which are more meaningful.

---

[3] For telling criticism of such theologies, see John Macquarrie, *God and Secularity* ("New Directions in Theology Today," III; Philadelphia: Westminster Press, 1967), pp. 81-85; Roger Lincoln Shinn, *Man: The New Humanism* ("New Directions in Theology Today," V; Philadelphia: Westminster Press, 1968), pp. 145-164.

Many priests rightly reacted to the poor obligationalism connected with the breviary and priestly prayer in the past. One can see here the evils of a legalistic system which tries to enforce itself in terms of penalties rather than educating the person to interiorly understand and embrace what the law is requiring. Once the penalty of the law was no longer meaningful, it was easy to forget about the whole reality of prayer. Obviously the purpose of the law was to provide for the prayer life of priests, but its legalistic approach prevented the law from accomplishing its purpose. There is no doubt that prayer requires some type of discipline. When all discipline had been brought about through external means of sanctions, then true education had not been accomplished. The result was a flip-flop in the opposite direction of no prayer at all. Prayer will always require some type of discipline, but this must be something which comes from the person's realization of its need and importance.

To read the signs of the times is always difficult, for one can never be sure that he is accurately understanding what is taking place. In the area of the prayer life of priests, it seems that many priests have given up the structured prayer of the past without putting too much in its place, but they are now searching for more meaningful ways of praying.

Prayer life is just one aspect of the spiritual life of the priest, for his prayer must be seen as an integral part of his service of the Word and Work of Jesus within the Christian community. In general there seems to be a feeling of malaise among many today. Perhaps the greatest source of this malaise is a sense of frustration which so often characterizes priests in their life and ministry today. Some have been frustrated because of various forms of authoritarianism in the Church as seen in their dealings with bishops, superiors or pastors. However, this situation, at least in many areas, seems to be slowly changing for the better.

A primary source of frustration comes not only from the crisis of identity but also from the lack of success in the ministry. In the warm afterglow of Vatican II renewal was the key word in the life of the Church. Hopes were high. Many changes had been brought about by the Council. The future prospects seemed almost unlimited. But the harsh reality of the last seven years has been much different. Renewal is not sudden or dramatic, nor does it occur easily and without struggle and difficulties. The euphoria of the last few years has quickly faded and often produced a real frustration and malaise. In many ways renewal within the Church has not been accomplished; in fact, it never will be totally accomplished.

Our ideas about the possibility of renewal were definitely romantic and naive. Catholic theology before Vatican II was rightly castigated for being triumphalistic about the Church. Theology did come to an appreciation of the sinful character of the Church and much of the old triumphalism was done away with. However, in a sense triumphalism of a new kind developed—a triumphalism of renewal which thought that renewal would come about quickly and easily. But renewal is much more than just statements or changing language in the liturgy. Renewal also calls for a renewal of structures which is always a long, arduous project. Above all renewal calls for our own change of hearts. If we are honest with ourselves, we realize that we do not change that easily. Change even in our personal lives is slow and often tortuous. The frustration which characterizes many priests today was only increased by the romantic expectations for renewal within the Church.

The rising expectations of the early 1960's have been frustrated not only in the ecclesial community but also in secular society. In the 1960's priests and the Church rightly began to take a more active role in the life of society, especially in the struggle for justice and peace. The March on Selma was a thrilling experience for all who participated in it, but the euporia of the early period of the civil rights movement has given way to the frustrations, bitterness and polarity that characterize society today. Some have become so frustrated that they have become alienated from all forms of our contemporary society. Perhaps the peace movement can take credit for the slow change in the attitude of the people of the United States to the war in Southeast Asia, but the length of the struggle and its harshness have not been encouraging for those who would work for the reform of society and its institutional structures. There is no doubt that much of this frustration is a reaction to the overoptimism of the early 1960's.

The mood of the early 1960's emphasized the power and responsibility that man had to renew and change his life. Progress seemed not only possible but also inevitable. Within a short time we could accomplish this change. The optimistic bubble of the early 1960's burst in the light of the harsh realities that became even more evident as the decade progressed. Poverty, prejudice and war were not overcome; in fact, they probably became stronger. Theology itself tended to follow too blindly the prevailing feeling of the contemporary culture so that it often failed to critically come to grips with what was happening.

In general, theology forgot the reality of sin and the reality of transcendence. The tendency to forget sin is perennial in the history of Christian thought and is especially evident in the more optimistic periods of human history. Today theology is striving to recover the proper sense of sin. For Catholics the reality of sin had been warped by a legalistic, minimalistic, and too one-sided approach to sin with its emphasis on personal and sexual morality. But when that concept of sin was jettisoned, nothing was put in its place. Today there is an attempt to see the full reality of sin with its personal, social and cosmic aspects. The recognition of human sinfulness does not call for a pessimism but rather a sober realism. Sin does now and always will exist despite our failure and unwillingness at times to recognize it. But the Christian is called to cooperate with Christ in the struggle against sin.

Likewise theology today is recovering its sense of the transcendent and mystery. Theologies of the future and theologies of celebration plus a renewed emphasis on the God question are all evidences of this fact. In many ways theologies of revolution or liberation can also be seen as signs of transcendence, but often there is involved that naive optimism which fails to realistically assess the situation and the possibilities. However, even in this area later writings have avoided some of the romanticism of revolution found in earlier writings.

This more sober assessment of the situation both in the Church and in the world, without giving in to a false quietism or acceptance of the status quo, should at least help to explain the frustration which many Christian ministers experience today. In a sense frustration will always be present in the work of the ministry, for all of us fall short of the gospel ideal to which we are called.

The very crisis of identity in the priestly ministry and the causes underlying it also contribute to the present feeling of malaise among so many priests. Especially older priests who were comfortable in their roles have now felt the anxiety brought about by changing understandings and structures. Some will struggle against the changes. Others find themselves unable to cope with the changes despite good will and tend to think about retirement. Even those who are searching for newer approaches feel somewhat uncomfortable and experience the lack of security.

Questioning and searching characterize the attitude of many priests today. Radical questioning is at the heart of many of the crises in contemporary life. The security of the past, which was frequently a false sense of security and ultimately immature, is gone. This questioning is intensified by the fact that many other priests including friends have chosen to leave the active ministry. This is bound to have an unsettling effect. However, this radical questioning and searching does not necessarily produce satisfactory answers.

THE EXAMPLE OF PAUL

As part of this search for a priestly spirituality I would propose the example of Paul the Apostle. Especially in the light of my reading of the signs of the times the model of Paul is particularly appropriate. The very heart of the renewal of Catholic theology in the period immediately before Vatican II was the return to the Scriptures. Contemporary theology while realizing the importance of the Scriptures also understands the limitations and shortcomings of the Scriptures precisely because they are culturally and historically conditioned documents. There are also different approaches and emphases even within the Scriptures themselves so that one scriptural witness must always be seen in the light of the whole scriptural witness.[4] As pointed out in the first chapter in a matter such as ministry the Scriptures say little or nothing about the concrete way of exercising that ministry in the very different circumstances of our contemporary existence. With this general understanding of the Scriptures, this chapter will investigate what might be called the spirituality of Paul the Apostle and with certain modifications propose this as an important model for the spirituality of the priestly minister today.

---

[4] Edouard Hamel, S.I., "L'Écriture, âme de la théologie," *Gregorianum*, LII (1971), 511-535.

Stanislaus Lyonnet has written a very pertinent article entitled, "The Fundamental Law of the Apostolate Formulated and Lived by Saint Paul."[5] Lyonnet summarizes this model or law of the apostolate in one scriptural verse—2 Cor 12:9. This verse is found in the context of the discussion of the famous thorn in the flesh which Paul experienced and which Lyonnet interprets in terms of some obstacle to his ministry.[6] Paul pleaded for this thorn in the flesh to be taken away- "But he has said, 'My grace is enough for you: my power is at best in weakness.' So I shall be very happy to make my weakness my special boast so that the power of Christ may stay over me." The following verse continues: "And that is why I am quite content with my weaknesses, and with insults, hardships, persecutions, and the agonies I go through for Christ's sake. For it is when I am weak that I am strong."[7]

Barnabas Ahern has in two companion essays, "The Power of His Resurrection," and "The Fellowship of His Sufferings," developed the theme of the paschal mystery as the basis of Pauline spirituality.[8] This is particularly true of the ministerial activity

---

[5] Stanislaus Lyonnet, "La loi fondamentale de l'apostolat formulée et vécu par saint Paul," in I. de la Potterie, S.J., and S. Lyonnet, S.J., *La Vie selon L'Esprit* (Paris: Editions du Cerf, 1965), pp. 263-282. An English translation has recently been published: *The Christian Lives by the Spirit* (Staten Island: Alba House, 1971). The development of Paul's understanding in this chapter depends especially on Lyonnet and two essays by Barnabas Ahern, C.P., mentioned below.

[6] *Ibid.,* pp. 265-266.

[7] Scriptural citations, unless otherwise noted, are from the *Jerusalem Bible.*

[8] Barnabas M. Ahern, C.P., *New Horizons* (Notre Dame, Ind.: Fides Publishers, 1963), pp. 75-131.

of the Apostle. The "power-weakness" theme of all God's activity applies with special force to the Christian who through his intimate union with the paschal mystery of Christ shares the death-life principle which leads the individual Christian and the whole body of Christians through suffering to glory. Ahern finds a perfect summary of this in Paul's letter to the Philippians: "The things that were gain to me, these, for the sake of Christ, I have counted loss. Nay more, I count everything loss because of the excelling knowledge of Jesus Christ, my Lord. For his sake I have suffered the loss of all things, and I count them as dung that I may gain Christ and be found in him, not having a justice of my own, which is from the Law but that which is from faith in Christ; the justice from God based upon faith; so that I may know him and the power of his resurrection and the fellowship of his sufferings" (Phil 3:7-10).[9]

There is a danger of choosing just those scripture texts which fit in with one's presuppositions and thus distort the real meaning of the teaching of the Scriptures. Obviously some selection and ordering will always be necessary, but theology must avoid a poor use of Scripture which looks only for proof texts seen in isolation from the whole scriptural data. This danger has been present in Catholic theology in the past and still shows itself especially in the area of spirituality. The theme of the Christian life and apostolate as a sharing in the paschal mystery of Jesus by which we suffer and die in order

---

[9] This is the scriptural translation cited by Ahern, p. 94.

to live the life of the resurrection is not just an isolated theme found occasionally in the writings of
Paul, but rather appears to be very important and
central to his own thinking.

This theme appears constantly in Second Corinthians which above all contains Paul's explanation
and defense of his own ministry. In the very beginning of the letter Paul thanks God the Father of Our
Lord Jesus Christ who comforts us in all our afflictions. Just as we share abundantly in Christ's sufferings, so through Christ we share abundantly in his
comfort too. Paul then recalls his own sufferings
and unbearable afflictions which forced him to rely
not on himself but on God who raises the dead.

In the fourth chapter Paul comments that we
have this treasure in earthen vessels to show that the
transcendent power belongs to God and not to us.
Paul then develops the meaning of this sharing in
the sufferings, death and resurrection of Jesus in his
own life and apostolate:

> We are in difficulties on all sides, but never cornered;
> we see no answer to our problems, but never despair;
> we have been persecuted, but never deserted;
> knocked down but never killed; always, wherever we
> may be, we carry with us in our body the death of
> Jesus, so that the life of Jesus, too, may always be
> seen in our body. Indeed, while alive, we are con-
> signed to our death every day, for the sake of Jesus
> so that in our mortal flesh the life of Jesus, too, may
> be openly shown. So death is at work in us, but life
> in you (2 Cor. 4:8-12).

The message of the living out of the paschal mystery in the apostolate continues to be the dominant

theme throughout Second Corinthians. Paul insists that we prove ourselves to be servants of God by great fortitude in times of suffering, distress and hardship. We are thought to be most miserable, but in fact are always rejoicing (2 Cor 6:1-10). Paul reminds his hearers that suffering in God's way means changing for the better and having no regrets, but to suffer, as the world knows suffering, brings death (2 Cor 7:10).

In the twelfth chapter Paul develops the theme of power in weakness which Lyonnet takes to be the fundamental law for the apostolate in the life of Paul. In the final chapter Paul returns again to the same theme. "You want proof, you say, that it is Christ speaking in me: you have known him not as a weakling, but as a power among you? Yes, but he was crucified through weakness, and still he lives now through the power of God. So then, we are weak as he was, but we shall live with him, through the power of God, for your benefit" (2 Cor 13:3-4).

Thus there can be no doubt about the importance which Paul attaches to the theme of power in weakness, joy in suffering, life in death, all in the light of union with the paschal mystery of Jesus. However, it is also true that this theme does not appear that strongly in the early writings of Paul. In the two letters to the Thessalonians the emphasis is more on resurrection-parousia rather than death-resurrection. These earlier letters do mention the need for suffering in the Christian life, but suffering is seen in terms of the struggle in the midst of the messianic tribulations which then becomes a pledge of salva-

ion at the time of the parousia or the second
coming.[10]

There has been an obvious development in Paul's
own thinking about the place of suffering in the life
of the Christian and the way in which it unites the
individual Christian to Christ Jesus. In Second
Corinthians as contrasted with Thessalonians, Paul
frequently links his own sufferings, which are
primarily those of his own apostolate, with the
paschal mystery. An important emphasis in the last
chapter was that contemporary theology has become more inductive and depends, although not entirely, on the lived experience of the individual.
Paul developed his thinking on the meaning of the
Christian life through his reflection on the meaning
of Jesus in the light of his own personal experience.
Fortunately we do have some record of Paul's experiences in the ministry, and these should be helpful in indicating how Paul came to formulate and
live the fundamental law of Christian ministry.

PAUL'S OWN EXPERIENCE

In the minds of many Christians Paul is the most
famous and the most successful figure in the history
of the Christian apostolate and ministry. There is
always a natural tendency to glorify the life of any
great figure and to forget about the problems and
difficulties which were part of that life. The Acts of
the Apostles presents us an aspect of Paul's life and

---

[10] Ahern, p. 97.

ministry which is not often remembered. In reality Paul's ministry was not a smashing success, but he knew and experienced failure, opposition, persecution and by his own admission even came close to despair. This experience was of great importance in Paul's self-understanding of the life of the Christian minister.

Chapter 16 of Acts describes what has traditionally been called the second missionary journey of Paul. The journey begins amid a difficult situation for Paul. Paul and Barnabas had been working together in the apostolate, and they were planning to go back and revisit the places in which they had preached the gospel. Barnabas wanted to take John Mark with them again, but Paul refused because John Mark had deserted them before in Pamphylia. The Lucan narrative speaks of a violent quarrel between Paul and Barnabas, and Paul then split off from Barnabas and chose Silas as his companion (Acts 15:36-40). A contemporary observer can wryly remark that the first team ministry in the Christian apostolate to the Gentiles ended in total failure. Two saints could not get along with one another! Such a realistic understanding helps to dispel the naive romanticism of some when talking about newer forms of ministry in the Church. There will always be personality frictions among the preachers of the gospel. The example of Paul in this case does remind us of the very human problem in his own ministry but also his determination to carry on despite these problems and to try again.

Paul passed through Asia Minor and for the first time preached the good news in what is now a part of Europe. Paul's preaching at Philippi was quite successful at first, until he cured a slave girl who had been possessed by an evil spirit because of which she had made much money for her owners. The owners took revenge by hauling Paul and Silas before the magistrates and having them flogged and thrown into prison. Paul and Silas were miraculously delivered from prison, but ultimately they left the area and came to Thessalonika where there was a Jewish synagogue (16:6-40).

Again there was some initial success, but some people were resentful and stirred up the crowd against them. When it was dark Paul and Silas went away to Beroea where they received a welcome hearing from the people in the synagogue. But the Jews from Thessalonika heard about Paul's success and were about to stir up the people so it was arranged for Paul to go away to Athens: In Athens Paul was again favorably received in the beginning. Paul's famous speech before the Council of the Areopagus and the reaction is recorded in Acts 17: 22-34. People have rightly acclaimed the technique in Paul's talk, for he started his preaching about Jesus by referring to the monument the Athenians had built to the unknown God. This was Jesus whom he was talking about. However, at the mention of the resurrection and rising from the dead, many of his hearers were no longer interested. Paul then, without any great success, left Athens and went to Corinth.

In his First Letter to the Corinthians Paul recalls how he felt when he first came to them. This feeling of Paul expressed in the second chapter is again seen in the context of the language of the cross which may be illogical to those who are not on the way to salvation, but the followers of Christ see the cross as the power to save. God has used the wisdom of the cross to show up human wisdom. "Here are we preaching a crucified Christ, to the Jews an obstacle that they cannot get over, to the pagans madness, but to those who have been called, whether they are Jews or Greeks, a Christ who is the power and wisdom of God. For God's foolishness is wiser than human wisdom, and God's weakness is stronger than human strength" (1 Cor 1:23-25).

> As for me, brothers, when I came to you, it was not with any show of oratory or philosophy, but simply to tell you what God had guaranteed. During my stay with you, the only knowledge I claimed to have was about Jesus, and only about him as the crucified Christ. Far from relying on any power of my own, I came among you in great "fear and trembling" and in my speeches and the sermons that I gave, there were none of the arguments that belong to philosophy; only a demonstration of the power of the Spirit. And I did this so that your faith should not depend on human philosophy but on the power of God (1 Cor 2:1-5).

The narrative of Acts describes how again in Corinth Paul began to experience opposition and frustration in his apostolate. Obviously this opposition was a trying experience for Paul, since he had been constantly running into such a pattern. But it is at Corinth that he is reported to have had a vision. In the vision the Lord spoke to him: "Do not be afraid to speak out nor allow yourself to be silenced: I am with you" (Acts 18:9).

This was the lesson which Paul came to learn in the course of his own ministry. The success of his apostolate did not depend primarily on his efforts and tangible results. Above all, his own commitment to the ministry and apostolate could not depend on his success and what he accomplished. The source of his personal commitment and the source of his hope was the power of God. Through his own experience in the apostolate Paul came to know the meaning of the paschal mystery. It is only through suffering that we find life. Paul thus understood the paradox of the Christian life and ministry as being power in weakness, joy in sorrow and life in death.

In the light of this experience Paul came to his understanding of the Christian life and ministry which he enunciated in terms of union with the paschal mystery. This chapter will now try to synthesize and systematize Paul's understanding of the paschal mystery which he came to see as the fundamental law of the Christian life and apostolate.

PAUL'S TEACHING ON THE PASCHAL MYSTERY

In the Pauline understanding the existence of Christ can be divided into two phases, one marked by his death but the other marked by his resurrection. But even more importantly, for Paul there is an intimate connection between the two phases in the life of Christ.[11] It is only natural that Paul who

---

[11] F. X. Durwell, *The Resurrection: A Biblical Study* (New York: Sheed and Ward, 1960), p. 40. This idea which Durwell develops at great length is summarized in the following paragraphs.

first experienced Jesus as the Risen Lord should build his own understanding of Christ around the resurrection.[12]

In many ways the death of Jesus was the natural culmination of life according to the flesh which he assumed. He took upon himself the sinful human condition, but the reality of sin in the biblical mentality is intimately associated with death.[13] Note that in Romans 5 Paul maintains that it was through sin that death came into the world. Genesis itself sees death as resulting from sin. Sin is the separation from the author of life and thus of its very nature involves death.

Flesh also has a connection with sin and death in the Pauline understanding. Paul sometimes refers to the two phases in the life of Jesus as life in the flesh and life in the spirit or in power. For Paul flesh does not refer to the material or bodily part of man as distinguished from the spiritual or noncorporeal part of man. The terms flesh and spirit for Paul are not component parts of the dual nature of man (spiritual-material), but rather they refer to the whole man insofar as he is under the power of the living spirit or the power of sin. Just as the spirit is intimately associated with life (note that the Creed refers to the Spirit as the giver of life), so the flesh is intimately connected with death. Thus sin and the flesh are intimately connected with death.

---

[12] David Michael Stanley, *Christ's Ressurection in Pauline Soteriology* ("Analecta Biblica," 13; Rome: Pontifical Biblical Institute, 1961), p. 250.

[13] Stanislaus Lyonnet, S.J., *De Peccato et Redemptione* I (Rome: Pontifical Biblical Institute, 1957).

Paul also sees the reality of the law as intimately connected with sin, flesh and death. Paul vehemently denies the rather crass conclusion that the law is sin and even gives an apology for the law as something good, holy and just in itself (Rom 7:12). But, nevertheless, the law has become intimately connected with the reality of sin and death. Sin used the law to bring about death. Thus sin, flesh and the law are all intimately associated with death. Since he naturally assumed these realities, in a true sense, Jesus had to die. "Death was therefore the culmination of Christ's carnal existence; it did not of itself abolish that existence but was its final goal. For every man it is simply the final consequence of the life of the flesh, the declaration of the dominion of sin, the sanction of the law's rule. Far from abolishing tyranny and servitude, it marks their highest point."[14]

Although in one sense the death of Jesus marked the victory of the power of death, sin, flesh and the law, this is only one side of the total picture. For the eyes of faith this was a redemptive death as seen through the resurrection. The resurrection marks the victory of life over death and all its powers. Jesus died because of sin but he also died to sin. The same is true of the flesh and the law—understood in the Pauline sense. His paschal mystery was the triumph of life over death, of the spirit over flesh and the ultimate demise of the law as a force connected with sin and death.

The paschal mystery as understood by Paul thus

---

[14] Durwell, p. 49.

shows the death-resurrection character of the life of Christ. His way to glory, power and life was in and through suffering and death. Through his redemptive love death itself was transformed. The one and the same reality, the death of Jesus, took on a double meaning. On the one hand it appeared to be the triumph of the powers of evil and death, but on the other hand it marked the ultimate demise of these powers. His movement towards life, glory and power was through death, humiliation and weakness. Through his obedience to the Father and his love for man, his death was redemptive. In the apparent weakness and defeat of death he brought about the victory and life of the resurrection.

Paul assigns the agency of the resurrection above all to the work of the Father and also gives an important role especially regarding others to the Spirit. Only once (1 Thess 4:14) does Paul say that "Christ arose," and this could very well be a citation from an ancient credal formula.[15] Elsewhere Paul invariably employs the expression that Christ was raised, sometimes explicitly mentioning the agency of the Father, and other times not (e.g., 1 Cor 15:4; 12:20; 2 Cor 5:15; Rom 4:25; 7:4). "Paul's originality, however, lies in his attribution of Christ's resurrection to God as Father both of Christ and of the Christians."[16] Paul also speaks of the Spirit in connection with the resurrection but especially the agency of the Spirit in the resurrection of Christians. "And if the Spirit of him who raised Jesus

---

[15] Stanley, p. 261.
[16] *Ibid.*

from the dead is living in you, then he who raised Jesus from the dead will give life to your own mortal bodies through his Spirit living in you" (Rom 8:11). Paul looks upon the giving of the Spirit as the characteristic activity of the risen Christ, and at times even identifies (e.g., Rom 8:9-10; 1 Cor 15:45) the Spirit's operation with the risen Christ. It is through the gift of the Spirit that Christians share in the new life of the resurrection.

Above all, the Christian participates in the paschal mystery of Christ through baptism. Through the outpouring of the Spirit in baptism the Christian is incorporated into the mystery of Christ with its twin aspects of death and life. "You have been taught that when we were baptized in Christ Jesus we were baptized in his death, in other words when we were baptized we went into the tomb with him and joined him in death, so that as Christ was raised from the dead by the Father's glory, we too might live a new life" (Rom. 6:2-4). The Christian in baptism dies with Christ to sin and death and thus shares in the newness of the life of the resurrection. Through baptism the Christian becomes a part of the new creation.

The baptismal incorporation into the death and resurrection of Christ thus becomes a principle of the moral life for the Christian. The reference to baptism in Romans 6 shows very well this moral purpose. Paul raises and then refutes the objection that we should remain in sin so that the grace of God may abound. He appeals to the fact that in baptism we have crucified our old selves with him to free ourselves from the slavery of sin and death.

We are to live out our baptism by continuing to die to sin so that we might share all the more in the life of the resurrection. Ceslaus Spicq describes the Christian life as a symbiosis with the Lord—the double rhythm of death and resurrection experienced like a stigmata marks the whole existence of the Christian. The Christian in his daily existence thus is called upon to live out the reality of his baptism.[17]

Especially in Romans and Galatians Paul affirms a connection between the suffering and death of Christ and the conflict and suffering in the daily life of Christians.[18] Again it is the same principle—the Spirit, who is working in Christ and in the individual Christian. Christian suffering is necessarily intimately connected with our union with Christ. Paul reminds us that through the Spirit we have become the children of God. And if we are children, we are also heirs of God and co-heirs with Christ sharing his sufferings so as to share his glory. What we suffer in this life cannot be compared with the glory that is yet to come (Rom 8:17,18). Paul's understanding of suffering in the Christian life has been frequently referred to as a mysticism of suffering.[19] Paul tells the Galatians that he bears the marks of the Lord Jesus in his body (Gal 6:17). In the course of his life he continually experiences in his body the death of

---

[17] Ceslaus Spicq, O.P., *The Trinity and Our Moral Life According to Saint Paul* (Westminster, Md.: Newman Press, 1963), pp. 45-46.

[18] Ahern, pp. 110ff.

[19] Alfred Wickenhauser, *Pauline Mysticism: Christ in the Mystical Teaching of Paul* (New York: Herder and Herder, 1960), p. 154.

the Lord Jesus Christ (1 Cor 15:31; 2 Cor 4:11). Even when speaking of his own sufferings, he often refers to them simply as the sufferings of Christ (Phil 3:10; Col 1:24; 2 Cor 1:5).

Thus for Paul the Christian in his daily life is so united with the paschal mystery that he co-suffers with Christ as the way to life and glory. The mystical union of the Christian with Christ becomes an imperative for the Christian to live out his life as a co-suffering, co-dying, co-burial and co-rejoicing with Christ. It is interesting to note that in the Pauline thought this union with Christ is with the paschal mystery and not with any particular aspects of the historical sufferings of the historical Jesus. Only occasionally does Paul mention these historical sufferings of Jesus. Paul does not, however, see this union with Christ in terms of union with historical actions of Jesus such as co-fasting and co-praying with Jesus. Paul does not develop a spirituality similar to that of the stations of the cross whereby the sufferings of the Christian are seen in relation to the concrete sufferings of Jesus in his historical passion. Paul centers the whole Christian life on the mystical union with the paschal mystery of Christ which takes place in baptism and becomes the imperative for the Christian life.[20]

Through his own personal experience and through reflection on the meaning of life in Christ Jesus, Paul the Apostle came to see the frustrations, persecutions, oppositions and failures of his own ministry as above all a sharing in the death and resurrection

---

[20] Ahern, pp. 112-114.

of Christ. His own sufferings in the apostolate actually brought him into closer union with the mystery
of Christ. Paul thus realized the great paradox that
in the midst of weakness there was power, in the
midst of death there was life and in the midst of sorrow and suffering there was joy. Redemptive union
with Christ changes the real meaning of suffering
and death. Death and life are continually at work
in our own lives. The mystery of the cross changes
what appears to be folly and death into wisdom and
life for those who believe. (1 Cor 1:17-19). The
death and resurrection of the Christian give a
Christocentric explanation based on the paschal
mystery to the general scriptural paradox of power
in weakness. The cross and death seem to be the
greatest sign of weakness and defeat, but in the eyes
of faith and vivified in Christian love the cross is the
sign of power, victory and life.

The sufferings and frustrations of his own ministry did not become a source of total discouragement
for Paul even though his own life indicates how
many sufferings he endured. One can well believe
that often he was on the brink of despair. But in
2 Corinthians especially Paul explains that he came
to see these as a share in the sufferings and death of
Christ and therefore not reasons for despair but for
hope. The power of God is made known in weakness, and life is present in death. The other Pauline
writings continue to develop this same theme, but
2 Corinthians is of special importance for our considerations because here Paul is talking about himself as a minister of the Word and Work of Jesus.
The same basic theme is quite central in Philip-

pians. Paul counts all other things as loss in comparison with knowing Christ Jesus. For Christ Paul will willingly lose all things. All that Paul desires is to know him and the power of his resurrection and the fellowship of his sufferings. It is only by sharing in Christ's sufferings and death that Paul will attain the resurrection from the dead (Phil 3:10-11).

One can well appreciate how Paul came to develop his understanding of the spirituality of the apostolate. As a minister of the Word and Work of Jesus he was above all a man of faith who saw reality in terms of the paschal mystery of Christ. It was this reality that gave ultimate meaning and support to his ministry. In this context suffering and frustration had a deeper meaning which was hidden except to the eyes of faith. His own commitment did not depend on the external success of his own accomplishments, but rather he came to see the true meaning of his sufferings and the difficulties of his own apostolate in terms of the paschal mystery of Jesus. Paul thus reveals the source of strength in his own apostolate and leaves a powerful example for all those who would dedicate themselves to preaching the gospel.

Too often we tend to glorify the lives of others and to forget the problems and difficulties in their lives. Paul came to realize that frustration and seeming failure would always be part and parcel of the Christian ministry. Whoever expects a ministry without such difficulties does not truly understand the meaning of the Christian ministry. Paul found his joy, hope and consolation not primarily in the success of his ministry but rather in the realization that his failures and sufferings were paradoxically the way in which he came to know the power of the Risen Lord.

THE WIDER CONTEXT OF THE SAME TEACHING

Paul thus understood the working of God in this world and in human events in terms especially of the paradox of power in weakness which in the light of the Christ mystery he interprets as a participation in the suffering, death and resurrection of Jesus. The Pauline paradox of power in weakness and life in death is not novel with him but stands as quite important in the whole development of the religious understanding of the people chosen by Yahweh.

The true clients of Yahweh in the Old Testament were called the poor of Yahweh, and the spirituality of the 'anawim became a characteristic spirituality of the Old Testament.[21] The poor of Yahweh were the people who gradually learned to place their trust, hope and confidence in Yahweh and in nothing else. There was a constant temptation for God's people to find their security in other things— gold, land, chariots, horses, alliances with powerful neighbors. However, in the course of history Israel was brought to the realization that these could never be the source of her strength. The lesson was hard and difficult, for God's people were stripped of all they had and ultimately were even exiled from

---

[21] Albert Gelin, P.S.S., *the Poor of Yahweh* (Collegeville, Minn.: Liturgical Press, 1963).

their own country which had been promised to them. Gradually they came to learn that their hope and their strength lay not in these things but in Yahweh and his power and his promise to them. They were truly a people of hope.

Human reverses and failures were the means chosen by God to bring his people to the realization that redemption and salvation would come as God's loving gift to man. The poor man, who has been stripped of all his possessions and then confidently with outstretched arms looks to God with faith and hope, is a great model of Old Testament spirituality. Through suffering his people came to distrust all human things and place their hope in Yahweh. The spirituality of the poor of Yahweh is often understood in terms of humility, for the poor in spirit are those who have learned through suffering and privation that their confidence rests not in possessions but in the gift of God and his saving power.

Later in the development of the Old Testament there appears the mysterious suffering servant who points to the Messias of the 'anawim (Is 52:13-53:12). Psalm 22 is definitely in the line of the spirituality of the 'anawim, and many Christians have given it a Christological interpretation. Jesus himself surely lived the life of the humble and suffering servant Messiah. His words reported on the cross in terms of the opening lines of Psalm 22—"My God, My God, why have you forsaken me?"—must be interpreted in the light of the suffering Messiah and the spirituality of the poor of Yahweh.

This is not a cry of despair on the part of Jesus or a feeling of dereliction as has often been proposed in Christian preaching. The first words of the psalm in the mouth of Jesus obviously call to mind the entire psalm. This psalm had developed perhaps by the fourth century into a liturgical psalm of thanksgiving. A later addition of some verses only strengthened the meaning of the psalm as the way in which the rule and righteousness of Yahweh operate. The success of the divine plan was seen as brought about through suffering and redemptive sacrifice. The ideal of this psalm was expressed by those who came to live in their own lives the spirituality of the poor of Yahweh. On the lips of Jesus it is primarily the cry of the Messiah confidently affirming that he would complete his work. It is the prayer of the just man who knows that in the midst of the necessary suffering the God of righteousness would protect him and accomplish the divine plan.[22] The psalm realizes that God will not despise or disdain the poor man, nor hide from him his face but rather will answer his call. Thus men will proclaim the Lord to generations still to come and will teach his righteousness to a people yet unborn (Psalm 22: 25-31).

The basic spirituality of the poor of Yahweh thus includes the theme of power in weakness and glory through suffering which became so central in the spirituality of Paul the Apostle. This basic theme is true not only of the Old Testament as a whole, but is also illustrated in many ways in the principal characters of the Old Testament. Obviously Abra-

---

[22] *Ibid.*, 84-88.

...am, the man of faith, represents this type of spirituality. His trust and confidence rested on the promise of God even when it seemed impossible from a human viewpoint for this promise to be fulfilled. He was to be the father of a great people and his offspring would be as numerous as the sands of the sea even though his wife was old and sterile. Despite apparent human impossibility God would still achieve his plan.

Lyonnet uses the example of Gedeon to illustrate dramatically the theme of God's power made known in human weakness.[23] God purposely reduces the size of Gedeon's troops so they number only 300. Yahweh does this to make sure that Gedeon and the people do not think that they have overcome the enemy with their power. In this way it will be very evident to them that it is the power of God working here. They are only instruments in the hands of God who will bring about his plan through his power (Jg 7:1-25).

Moses and David would also be excellent examples of how God used the weak and the apparently powerless to bring about his plan. The reality of the suffering servant motif which grows out of this spiritual milieu can be seen in the lives of the prophets, especially Jeremiah. Jeremiah realized his weakness, the thanklessness of his task and the suffering it would entail; but in the midst of this ministry he also experienced the power of God. Job is another Old Testament figure who

---

[23] Lyonnet, *La Vie selon L'Esprit*, pp. 274-275.

stands as an example of the spirituality of those who
through suffering came to know the saving power
of God.[24]

A CONTEMPORARY EXAMPLE

Paul's experience thus is in general continuity
with a theme that runs throughout the Scriptures
and was seen especially in the life and death of
Jesus. Obviously this type of spirituality has continued to flourish in Christianity and especially
among ministers of the gospel. One particular contemporary example is most illuminating for the
priestly minister. Yves Congar proposes this Pauline
spirituality of the paschal mystery for the priestly
minister today. This spirituality is evident in
Congar's own life and is proposed by him in a very
touching article in the form of a letter to his brother
priests.[25]

Congar too detects a general feeling of discouragement existing among many priests today. Congar
attributes this to the fact that the priest is isolated
and not understood both in the world and in the
Church. So often in the world today people are not
interested in his mission and function and cannot
appreciate what he is trying to do. Many priests also
feel isolated in the Church community because they
cannot communicate with their bishop, and even
members of the Church do not really understand

---

[24] Gelin, pp. 46-50.
[25] Yves M.-J. Congar, O.P., "A mes frères prêtres," *La Vie
Spirituelle,* CXIII (1965), 501-520.

what they are trying to do. Many priests are questioning the meaning and results of their ministry.[26] In this state of discouragement brought about by isolation and loneliness, Congar counsels a response of faith and hope.

Perhaps this response of faith and hope in the midst of failure, discouragement and lack of understanding is best illustrated in Congar's own life and spirituality. Congar merely alludes to his own life at the beginning of his letter to his brother priests. He is conscious of addressing his letter to his brothers who are in pain and often suffering in the extreme; whereas he personally has security, is engaged in interesting work, is praised by other men and acclaimed as being successful. While admitting this to be true, Congar adds that he has known difficult hours, opposition, solitude and even exile coupled with the horrible temptation of thinking that the dark night would never end.[27]

Elsewhere, Congar has somewhat reluctantly reflected on the circumstances of his own life. This reflection forms the long preface to his book *Chrétiens en dialogue* published in 1964.[28] One rather large segment of this preface deals with his life from 1939 to the end of the 1950's, and he captions this period in his life as a time for patience.[29] Just the barest

[26] *Ibid.,* pp. 502-506.

[27] *Ibid.,* p. 501.

[28] Yves M.-J. Congar, O.P., "Preface: Appels et cheminements: 1929-1963," in *Chrétiens en dialogue* (Paris: Éditions du Cerf, 1964), pp. IX-LXIV. Subsequent references will be to the English translation: *Dialogue Between Christians,* tr. Philip Loretz (Westminster, Md.: Newman Press, 1966).

[29] *Ibid.,* pp. 28-44.

of descriptions indicates that Congar in his own ministry was a man who knew and lived the spirituality of the paschal mystery. In April of 1939 he was called to Paris along with his teacher and friend, Father Chenu, and informed of some problems and difficulties connected with his book, *Chrétiens désunis.* However, the war intervened, and Congar spent much of that time in prison. It was in prison that he learned the Saulchoir, the institution with which he was associated and the center for theological renewal in the Dominican order, had been struck a mortal blow by Church authorities. After the war he eagerly joined in the theological renewal which was taking place in France, but his path was frequently blocked. "As far as I myself am concerned, from the beginning of 1947 to the end of 1956 I knew nothing from that quarter [Rome] but an uninterrupted series of denunciations, warnings, restrictive or discriminatory measures and mistrustful interventions."[30]

In March of 1947 one article was disapproved of; another totally suppressed. A meeting of Catholic ecumenical workers had to be abandoned. In December of 1947 he was forbidden to publish a paper on the position of the Catholic Church toward ecumenism, which he had been requested to write by the World Council of Churches in preparation for their meeting in Amsterdam in 1948. Meanwhile, he was reworking his book *Chrétiens désunis* for a new edition. The Father General of the Dominicans took it for censoring, kept it for two years, and re-

---

[30] *Ibid.,* 34.

urned it with such vague suggestions for changes
hat it was impossible for Congar to publish the
)ook. His *True and False Reform in the Church* was
irst published in France in 1950, but in 1952 all
urther printings and translations of the book were
orbidden. Recall that at this time the encyclical
Humani Generis was issued by Pope Pius XII in an
•ffort to stem the so-called new theology. "I was told
o submit all my writings to Rome and this I
lid after February 1952, down to the smallest review. I remember it all very well and my recollec-
ions are confirmed by the manuscripts which I have
‹ept, which show the incredible narrowness of the
:ensorship as well as the great care devoted to it by
ny distant colleagues."[31]

1953 was a dark year for the Dominican order in
France. Three provincials of France were removed.
Most of the important Dominican theologians were
•xiled—Congar going to Jerusalem. In Jerusalem
ne wrote *The Mystery of the Temple,* and he laconi-
:ally remarks that seven censors took three years to
lecided to permit its publication. He was called to
Rome in September 1954, and after a few months
)f waiting was exiled again—this time to Cam-
)ridge in England where he was treated poorly in
nis own Dominican house. Only after his return to
France in 1956 did things begin to change.

After detailing the incidents of these painful
‹ears, Congar explains in a personal way his own
heology of the paschal mystery. His explanation is
nost moving.

[31] *Ibid.,* p. 40.

Anyone who is acquainted with me knows that I am impatient in little things. I am incapable of waiting for a bus! I believe, however, that in big things I am patient in an active way about which I would like to say a word here. This is something quite different from merely marking time. It is a quality of mind, or better of the heart, which is rooted in the profound, existential conviction, firstly that God is in charge and accomplishes his gracious design through us, and secondly that, in all great things, delay is necessary for their maturation. One can only escape the servitude of time in a time which is not void but in which something is happening, something the seeds of which have been confided to the earth and are ripening there. It is the profound patience of the sower who knows that "something will spring up" (cf. Zechariah 3:8; 6:12). I have often thought of the words of St. Paul; "Patience breeds hope" (Romans 5:4). One could wait patiently because he had hope in his heart. In a certain sense this is true, but the order in which St. Paul puts it reveals a more profound truth. Those who do not know how to suffer, do not know how to hope either. People who are in too much of a hurry, who wish to grasp the object of their desires immediately, are also incapable of it. The patient sower, who entrusts his seed to the earth and the sun is also the man of hope. Coventry Patmore has said that to the man who waits all things reveal themselves, provided that he has the courage not to deny in the darkness what he has seen in the light. . . .

If this patience is that of the sower, it is necessarily accompanied by a cross. "Those who sow in sorrow, reap in shouts of joy" (Psalm 126:5), but sometimes they do not reap at all, for "one sows and another reaps" (John 4:37). The cross is a condition of every holy work. God himself is at work in what to us seems a cross. Only by its means do our lives acquire a certain genuineness and depth. Nothing is meant wholly seriously unless we are prepared to pay the price it demands. "It belongs to the place in our poor hearts which is not even there until suffering has entered in" (L. Bloy). Only when a man has suffered for his convictions does he attain in them a certain force, a certain quality of the undeniable and, at the same time, the right to be heard and to be respected. *O crux benedicta* ("O blessed cross").[32]

One can only admire such a life and spirituality. And yet one can and perhaps must raise the question whether Congar should have endured all this. Perhaps reform would have been achieved more quickly if he would have resisted more actively or perhaps even left his ministry. Perhaps such a spirituality is too passive and too easily accepts the imperfections and sinfulness of the institution and people in it. There are times when one cannot passively suffer, but must speak out boldly and resist the wrong that is being done. Congar himself realizes there is no meaning in suffering just for the sake of suffering. Although one might raise questions about Congar's response, one can only admire the man and his spirituality. No matter how one measures success in the Christian life, it would seem in hindsight that Congar did the right thing.

To the priests of today experiencing loneliness and discouragement, Congar offers this type of spirituality. Although each minister humbly sows his seed in his own little corner of the world, he does

---

[32] *Ibid.*, pp. 44-45.

effect things that will never be known or appraised. A deeper appreciation of the Christian apostolate shows that it will always involve a dramatic struggle against what Paul calls the Powers. The power of God reveals itself in the weakness of man, and the minister of the gospel must share in the messianic sufferings. Congar then shows how Paul develops this spirituality in Second Corinthians. This is the wisdom of the cross which is not a dark pessimism, but which in the midst of suffering is sustained by the certitude of hope in the power of God and the life of the resurrection.[33]

Such a spirituality I believe is most important for a priest today especially in the midst of the malaise, discouragement, questioning, insecurity and searching which is so often a part of the life of priestly ministry today. This type of spirituality is not just something that corresponds to the signs of the times today but has also been present in all times and ages in the Church. It seems even more relevant and meaningful today.

However, one must properly understand this spirituality and see it in the whole context of the Christian life. Earlier mention was made of the danger of taking one aspect of the Christian life and so absolutizing it that the meaning is distorted. Likewise in the practical aspect one could question the strict application of this spirituality in all aspects of Christian life and ministry. In briefly discussing the exemplary ministry of Yves Congar this

---

[33] Congar, *La Vie Spirituelle*, CXIII (1965), 515-522. It is interesting to note that in developing this concept of spirituality Congar quotes extensively from Psalm 22.

question did arise. Just how should this important model of spirituality be nuanced and understood?

THEOLOGICAL COMPARISONS

It should be helpful to examine briefly how two contemporary theologians have dealt with the reality of the paschal mystery as central to Christian life and spirituality. These two different approaches illustrate two different ways of understanding the paschal mystery motif and will assist our search for a nuanced realization of this type of spirituality.

Dietrich Bonhoeffer sees the Christian moral life in terms of conformation with the unique form of Him who was made man, was crucified and rose again. Bonhoeffer shows the failure of any ethic based on reason, conscience, duty, responsibility or virtue, for they are all the achievements and attitudes of a noble humanity. But the judgment of God in the crucifixion rules out all these possible models of the ethical life for the Christian. The fact that God has become man eliminates both extremes of the idolization of man present in all the foregoing attempts to describe the moral life of the Christian and also the extreme that debases and scorns man.

The world thinks only in terms of success and equates the good with success, but the figure of the Crucified invalidates all thought which makes success the standard. Man is understood in terms of the judgment of God, which is expressed in the crucifixion and the resurrection. It is not totally a judgment of condemnation of man, for in the last analysis God pronounces on man a sentence of mercy.

Conformation with the crucified Christ does not come about by our own efforts, for in the last analysis it is Christ who shapes men in conformation with himself. Man then must live out this conformation with the crucified and risen Christ.[34]

Bonhoeffer's approach to the conformation with Christ in the moral life of the Christian is definitely in the somewhat Orthodox (as distinguished from the Liberal) Protestant tradition. In no sense does Bonhoeffer see the Christian life as building on the human and a development of the human. The crucifixion shows the grace of God as completely opposed to the sinful human condition. Thus Bonhoeffer rejects any theology that would build on the notions of reason, virtue, responsibility, etc. However, Bonhoeffer does not take an entirely negative view of man. The judgment of the crucifixion and resurrection is not a mere condemnation or "no" to everything human. The judgment of God is above all a merciful "yes" to man, but there is little to distinguish the new man from the rest of men.[35] Thus Bonhoeffer in his *Ethics* does not stress as much as some Lutheran theologians the negative judgment of God on man and the human.

Bernard Lonergan writing in the Catholic tradition also talks about the law of the cross. Lonergan proposes as a thesis that the Son of God was made man, suffered, died and was buried because divine wisdom ordained and the divine goodness willed

---

[34] Dietrich Bonhoeffer, *Ethics* (New York, Macmillan, 1965), pp. 3-25.

[35] *Ibid.*, p. 19.

not simply to take away the evils of the human race but according to the just and mysterious law of the cross to convert these same evils into the greatest good, which is the whole Christ, head and members in this world and in the future.[36] This just and mysterious law of the cross then becomes exemplary for all Christians.

However, there are many important differences between Bonhoeffer and Lonergan. Even notice the formulation of the thesis in Lonergan. He seems to admit a basic goodness about the human race but that it is infected with sin. The law of the cross shows the opposition between sin and grace (to use the older, technical term), but the human is not necessarily the opposite or even opposed to grace. Ultimately, as is most evident from his other writings Lonergan does not make sin as total and as all pervasive as does Bonhoeffer. Since the human for Lonergan is not practically identified with the sinful, it does not require such a total transformation or conversion. Lonergan sees grace and redemption in some continuity with the human and creation.

In general these two theologians illustrate the different approaches in Protestant and Catholic theological traditions which will have a bearing on this question of the law of the cross and the paradox of power in weakness and life in death. The Protestant tradition generally sees sin as affecting and almost absorbing the human so that man and reality with-

[36] B. Lonergan, S.I., *De Verbo Incarnato* (Rome: Pontifical Gregorian University, 1960), p. 676.

out the grace and gift of God are in total opposition to God and the things of God. This theology has generally stressed the transcendence of God and the weakness of man who in faith receives the gift of God for salvation.

The Protestant tradition is frequently associated with the formulas faith alone and grace alone. Catholic tradition is more associated with the formulas faith and reason, grace and works. The Protestant tradition accuses the Catholic tradition of so insisting on works that it forgets the basic reality of salvation as God's saving gift to man. At times some Catholics do seem to have fallen into this error. In theological reflection Protestant tradition does not give that much importance to man's reason and has tended to resist natural law and natural theology. The only true wisdom about God comes from revelation and not from reason.

There is a coherence in the different formulae of Scripture alone, faith alone, grace alone, found together in some forms of Protestant theology. The coherence comes from the basic thrust which emphasizes the transcendence of God and the sinfulness of man. There is no doubt that in places Paul certainly does tend to give evidence of favoring such an approach. Paul definitely emphasizes that man is saved through faith and not by works—a position all Christians should hold. Likewise in Paul sinfulness tends to be somewhat all pervasive. Paul tends to see all reality in terms of dichotomies. Man is either under sin or under grace; he is either living according to the flesh or according to the Spirit. If all reality is so dichotomized, then there is this great opposition between existing man and the loving God.[37]

The Catholic tradition has generally given less emphasis to the all pervasiveness of sin. Likewise it has not pictured God as so transcendent that he is totally unknowable and unapproachable for man. God reveals himself to us somewhat even in his creation, so that man in and through creation can come to know something about God. Thus Catholic theologians have developed a natural law and a natural theology as well as giving an important place to reason in theology. Lonergan really develops his whole system in terms of man's understanding of his own knowing process.[38] In his *Ethics* Bonhoeffer obviously rejects such an approach. Catholic theology thus sees greater continuity between nature and grace, between creation and redemption, between the human and the divine.

In the ethical and spiritual areas perhaps the best illustration of the difference in these two generic

---

[37] For a comparison between such a Protestant approach and a Catholic perspective, see from the Catholic perspective Franz Böckle *Law and Conscience* (New York: Sheed and Ward, 1966). As an example of a Lutheran position with frequent references to the opposite Catholic opinion, see Helmut Thielicke, *Theological Ethics,* Vol. 1: *Foundations,* ed. William H. Lazareth (Philadelphia: Fortress Press, 1966). It is necessary to point out that I am not referring to all forms of Protestant theology, but this generally applies to theology in the Barthian, and especially in the Lutheran tradition. In the United States there appears to be a greater convergence and agreement today on these questions than there is in Europe, at least as the European situation is described by Roger Mehl, *Catholic Ethics and Protestant Ethics* (Philadelphia: Westminster Press, 1971).

[38] Bernard J. Lonergan, S.J., *Insight: A Study of Human Understanding* (New York: Longmans, 1957).

approaches is shown in the understanding of Christian love. What is the precise relationship between Christian love or *agape* and human love? The strict Lutheran tradition would see a great difference and even an opposition between the two. *Agape* is strictly distinguished from *eros* or romantic love, which in this sense has nothing to do with sexuality but rather is the love of desire, and its happiness and fulfillment in the other. *Agape* is also distinguished from *philia* or friendship love which emphasized the mutuality and reciprocity of love. *Agape* is the love with which God has loved us and the love we try to show to others. The great characteristic of this love is that it is spontaneous and unmotivated; that is, in no way does it depend upon the object of the love. God loves us not because of anything in us or anything he might receive from us but only because of his own generous good will to offer us his love. *Agape* is the total willingness to give and is independent of the object of the love. Agape by its very nature excludes the idea of reciprocity or fulfillment.[39]

Anders Nygren well illustrates this approach to *agape*. *Agape* as the distinctive Christian love is quite different from, and even opposed to, human love. Any concept of fulfillment or reciprocity would belittle the true meaning of *agape*. Nygren argues strenuously against the Catholic tradition which has always tried to see *agape* as containing, employing and transforming human love. In

---

[39] Anders Nygren, *Agape and Eros* (New York: Harper Torchbook, 1969).

the Catholic tradition *agape* and human love are not opposed but rather *agape* brings human love to its fulfillment. Christian love somehow or other does and must include the notions of mutuality and fulfillment even though these might not be the primary elements in such a love.[40]

Nygren is critical of Augustine who in many ways is the most important early historical spokesman for this type of love. Augustine tries to combine *agape* and human love. Notice that Augustine uses the word *caritas* or charity to describe this Christian love for God which includes an element of happiness, fulfillment and reciprocity, because God has made us for himself and our hearts will not rest until they rest in him.[41] Here I would agree with the general thrust of the Catholic tradition which sees Christian love not as opposed to human love but as including all the elements of human love, but transforming them in the light of God's love.

I do theologize within the Roman Catholic theological tradition and thus reject the approach associated with more Orthodox forms of Protestantism. However, there also have been many unsatisfactory elements in Catholic theology in the past precisely in the area of sin and of relating creation and redemption or nature and grace. Catholic theology has tended not to give enough importance to the reality of sin and likewise has not seen grace and redemption as affecting and to some extent transforming the human.

---

[40] M. C. D'Arcy, S.J. *The Mind and Heart of Love* (New York: Meridian Books, 1956).

[41] Nygren, pp. 449-562.

Another important emphasis in Roman Catholic theology has been its understanding of justification as bringing about a real, ontological change in man. The grace of God truly changes man and makes him a new creature in Christ Jesus. The grace of God is thus seen to have real effects in man and in his world.[42] This efficacy of grace is seen from another viewpoint in the Catholic theology of the Church and of the sacraments. The grace of God is not something totally hidden and invisible, but it does bring about real changes and does become somewhat visible.

SOME IMPORTANT NUANCES

However, there are also many different theological approaches within Protestantism. I have been referring in general to an approach which has been present in the Lutheran tradition. Lutheran theology because of the reasons mentioned above can be called a dilectical or even a paradoxical theology. H. Richard Niebuhr considered much the same question being considered here in his book *Christ and Culture*. Niebuhr examines the different ways in which Christian theology has tried to understand the two realities of Christ and culture which is somewhat the same as the relationship between nature and grace. Niebuhr refers to the Lutheran tradition as Christ and culture in paradox; whereas he

---

[42] For a growing convergence even on justification between Barthian and Catholic thought, see Karl Rahner, "Controversial Theology on Justification," *Theological Investigations* (Baltimore: Helicon, 1966), IV, 189-218.

refers to the Augustinian position as Christ transforming culture.[43] He characterizes the position of
Thomas Aquinas and the Catholic position as Christ
above culture.[44] Note that my objections above to
some elements in the Catholic tradition would also
tend to argue for a Christ transforming culture approach. There are many Christian theologians today
both Protestant and Catholic who would tend to
find themselves somewhere in this category.

As imperfect as these categories are, they do serve
to give a general idea of the differences in approach
to the question of the spirituality of the paschal
mystery. The Lutheran approach, as is evident from
the description given by Niebuhr, definitely stressed
the notion of paradox. Paradox as the central theme
in theology would tend to see paradox as the regular
way in which God works with man and the world
so that his power is shown in weakness, joy in sorrow and life in death.

The more conversionist approach would have to
maintain that God does not always work this way.
Sometime the power of God is shown in power, and
the joy of God in human joy and the glory of God
in human glory, and the life of God in the life of
man. The conversionist motif, however, realizes
there is always a transcendent element because of
the inherent imperfections, limitations and sinfulness of the human. Sometimes this transcendence
is shown in the fact that God's power is made
known in human weakness, and joy in sorrow and

[43] H. Richard Niebuhr, *Christ and Culture* (New York:
Harper Torchbook, 1956), pp. 170-184; 190-229.
[44] *Ibid.*, pp. 120-148.

life in death. Since in Catholic thinking man is truly changed by his participation in the paschal mystery through baptism, the Christian is truly now belonging to the Father and has become a son with the Son. Consequently, the relationship of God to man cannot be seen primarily or only in terms of paradox.

The understanding of the moral implications of the paschal mystery with such a theological understanding would not always be in terms of a total paradox. The Christian already does belong to Jesus Christ, although there always remains some sinfulness. Conversion is a continual process which is modeled on the need to die to ourself and our sin so that we might rise in the newness of life. But man baptized in Christ Jesus is already in many ways joined with God in communion of love with him. Sin to some extent has already been overcome, but the Christian must struggle against it. Daily we must die to self but in this way we grow in the newness of life received in baptism.

In the light of the signs of the times, the scriptural data and theological reasoning I would still argue for the importance of a spirituality in the priestly ministry based on the paschal mystery. However, I would not see the God-man relationship totally in terms of paradox especially for the baptized Christian who is now sharing in the life and love of God in Jesus Christ. The conversionist motif does not have to understand the paschal mystery in terms of total paradox. The conversionist or continual growth motif stresses more the continuity in the development of the Christian life, but readily acknowledges the continuing sinfulness of the Christian. Thus growth itself follows a pattern of dying to sin and to self so that we might grow in life and love.

In many ways the crisis in spirituality in the ministry reflects the failure to appreciate the reality of transcendence both in theology and in the life of the Church in the early 1960's. The stress on immanence, the overoptimism and the emphasis on quick success in solving the complex problems of human existence both in the Church and in the world are all signs of the disregard of transcendence. Transcendence in the form of Christian eschatology reminds us that we are living between the two comings of Jesus. This type of eschatology in the process of realization is another expression of the conversionist motif. We have already risen with Christ in the newness of life in baptism, but the fullness of the eschaton has not yet come and will not come except outside history. In the meantime we continually fall short and experience the reality of our sinfulness and our failure to respond totally to God's gift.

The sixties suffered from the theological disease of an acute case of collapsed eschaton. Renewal minded Christians especially in the Catholic Church at the time of Vatican II thought that renewal would come about easily and quickly. The reality has been much harsher, and I hope it has made us all a little wiser. Unfortunately it has been a disillusioning experience for some, but it can and should serve as a sober reminder of the fact that in the times in between the comings of Jesus we continually fall short of the fullness of the gospel message and to that extent are always frustrated. The Christian believes that it is God in his saving power who will ultimately bring about the kingdom even though we are called upon to cooperate to a certain extent in this work.

Precisely for the foregoing reasons the paschal mystery understood in conversionist thought patterns lies at the heart of priestly spirituality. This means that all things are not understood only in terms of paradox. Sometimes God's glory is shown in human glory and God's goodness in human goodness. Human beauty is a sharing in God's beauty. Thus even in the Christian ministry one must find some success and some satisfaction in his work. Obviously, Paul the Apostle did find some fulfillment and human satisfaction in his apostolate. Especially in later years Congar has known the satisfaction of hearing Paul VI declare publicly that Congar was the one theologian who had influenced him the most. Even in his darkest days there was some satisfaction from his own intellectual growth and from the comfort and aid of friends.

The same is true for the priestly minister today. He needs to find some satisfaction in his apostolate, and there is always some satisfaction in the fact that we are helping and serving God's people. Since this spirituality does not deny the human, then all these things have a place in the spirituality of the priest. He needs the help, support, encouragement and sometimes the criticism of good friends. He needs the recreation of mind and body. He needs all the maturity that he can acquire. He needs, perhaps

especially, a sense of humor which in its own way
is a sign of transcendence. The person who cannot
laugh at himself is so involved with himself and his
work that he cannot stand back to see himself and
even laugh at some of the incongruities.

The spirituality of the priest above all consists in
knowing Jesus Christ and in putting on the Lord
Jesus Christ. The paschal mystery lies at the center
of the mystery of Christ. God, his love and his saving power are present in many different ways in all
that exists in this world. But the love and power of
God transcend all existing reality. The fullness of
the work of redemption has not yet come, and
despite our necessary cooperation, the kingdom is
ultimately God's saving gift to us. Thus to a certain
extent the love, power and presence of God are always incomplete and lie somewhat hidden in the
human. The minister of the Word and Work of Jesus
will also experience the reality of power in weakness
and joy in sorrow. This is one way in which the transcendence of God is manifested.

Likewise he must come to see the shortcomings,
frustrations, oppositions and even persecutions in
his own ministry as a sharing in the suffering and
death of Jesus and the way to the joy and glory of
the resurrection. The paschal mystery certainly includes aspects of paradox but it also includes other
ways in which the Christian who is in union with
Jesus shares in the love and mercy of the Father.
The Christian and the minister this side of the
eschaton will always fall short in his life and his
ministry. Such frustration is part and parcel of life
between the two comings of Jesus but should not be

a reason for demoralization; but rather in and through these, the minister learns that the law of growth or continual conversion for the Christian is patterned on the paschal mystery.

The priestly minister of the Word and Work of Jesus above all must be one who experiences his communion and life with Christ. This is at the core of his priestly ministry, the source of his joy and the strength of his commitment. He can depend on no other experience to take its place. There are many ways in which he can and should come into contact with the mystery of Christ. Obviously Christ is present in the people he serves and in his daily ministry, but the transcendent aspect of this mystery can never be perfectly expressed in the reality of the present. Realizing his own weaknesses and failures and the weaknesses of others he comes to see that the power of God transcends the present and looks with hope to the future as God's gift to us. Above all the priest must develop a prayer life which allows him to reflect on this reality which he knows in faith and hope. The priest like every Christian comes to learn that Christian conversion or growth follows the rhythm of the paschal mystery. The priest knows and experiences the mystery of the Christ he serves both in the fellowship of his sufferings and in the power of his resurrection.

III.

Crisis in Preaching the Word of God

A crisis in preaching appears to be a perennial reality if one can judge from the often heard complaints in this matter. This chapter will not deal with the whole scope of preaching. Nor will it discuss new and different formats for the homily, such as a dialogue homily, which can be a very effective means of communicating and sharing the Word of God. The concern here is not with techniques or means to improve the way in which the minister tries to communicate the Word of God to his people. This chapter will discuss the narrower but very important question of preaching the Word of God and its relationship to moral and social problems. There is a developing crisis in this area precisely because many people are in disagreement about the relationship between preaching the Word of God and the concrete moral and human problems of our lives.

THE PROBLEM

The minister of the Word and Work of Jesus knows both the privilege and the awesome responsibility of preaching the Word of God. The conscientious preacher of the Word realizes the trust committed to him and his consequent obligation to preach that Word and not another word. The preacher of the Word is familiar with scriptural warnings about false preachers and false teachers. The preacher of the Word also has an obligation and a trust to those he serves to be faithful to the Word and not to substitute his own word for the Word of God.

Problems of Christian morality only heighten the dilemma. What should the preacher or the homilist say, if anything, about contemporary moral problems and situations? Does he abuse his trust by talking to his congregation about the war in Southeast Asia? Does he remain quiet on the question of the bussing of school children as a means of bringing about a more integrated and just society? Does the Word of God as preached have anything to say about labor's right to strike, public housing developments to supply low cost housing, international relations with the Third World, organized crime, or inadequate welfare laws?

Special problems exist within the context of the Roman Catholic Church. Does the Church authority have the right to use the pulpit to speak against laws permitting abortion on demand? If the magisterium uses the pulpit in this case, are there other occasions and times for speaking out on other proposed legislation in the area of the rights of labor or any other issue? All the areas mentioned are questions of acute moral concern for Christians and for all mankind. But they are also areas in which there might be a variety of opinions existing within the Christian or the Catholic Church. In some places Christians and Catholics hold contradictory positions on these questions.

Many of these problems, especially those pertaining to the category of social and legal morality, involve a number of complex, prudential judgments requiring a great knowledge and expertise. Is it not audacious for the preacher of the Word to think that he knows more about these complex problems than the experts who have been studying them for years? Even if one could acquire expertise in one small area, this constitutes no solution at all, for there are so many important questions of this type. Once again the reality of complexity appears to lie at the heart of the crisis in this area.

The minister of the Word also has responsibilities to his congregation who expect him to preach the Word of God to them. There have been Christians on both sides of the question of the involvement of the United States in Southeast Asia. There are Christians who have fled their homeland to avoid serving in the conflict and like minded people who have been put in jail because of their protests and actions against the war. On the other hand, there have been Christians who have died in battle believing that they were not doing something which was appealing in any way but was a reluctant necessity in the world in which we live. Proponents of both points of view claim they are Christian and want the Word of God preached and ministered to them. Does this indicate that because of his responsibility to all those who believe in the Word of God —those who carry the signs of protest and those who wear the army uniform of their country—the minister of the Word would violate his mandate if he were to use the preaching office of the Word to become specific on the question of the morality of the American presence in Southeast Asia?

The complexity of many contemporary moral and social problems as well as the fact that Christians who look to us to preach the Word of God to them are basically divided on such issues might indicate that the preacher of the Word of God steps beyond his competence in commenting from the pulpit on specific issues of social morality. Perhaps he even thereby brings about a greater division and bitterness among the people of God, when he is commissioned to nourish them with the Word of God and work for the great Christian gift of reconciliation.

Yet if this position is taken, the Word of God remains somewhat general and thereby seemingly detached from the major questions facing the individual and society today. The Word of God seems once again to be divorced from the daily life of the Christian, and there seems to appear again that "split between the faith which many profess and their daily lives [which] deserves to be counted among the more serious errors of our age."[1] The *Pastoral Constitution on the Church in the Modern World* seems

---

[1] *Pastoral Constitution on the Church in the Modern World*, n. 44.

to appreciate the reality of the dilemma as proposed here. In its introductory statement the Council Fathers declare that "the Church has always had the duty of scrutinizing the signs of the times and of interpreting them in the light of the gospel."[2] Yet later on, the same document expresses a certain limitation: "The Church guards the heritage of God's Word and draws from it religious and moral principles, without always having at hand the solution to particular problems."[3]

Another dimension of the same dilemma is the relationship between so-called private and social morality. For years the Word of God has been addressed to rather specific problems of individual and personal morality such as sexuality, truth telling, stealing, killing and anger. If the Word of God has something to say in this area, should it not also have something to say in the area of social questions? In the first chapter it was pointed out that one of the deficiencies in the pastoral work of the Church has been a rather individualistic understanding of the mission of the Church and the failure to see the societal and cosmic dimensions of the Word and of the mission of Christians. Is there any real difference between individual moral questions and societal questions? Should we recognize any difference here or should the approach of the mission of the Church and the preacher of the Word be the same in both areas?

The above paragraphs try to present the most pressing problem raised by the preaching of the

---

[2] *Ibid.*, n. 4.
[3] *Ibid.*, n. 33.

Word of God in moral matters. However, there are other problems too, which in a sense participate in this same basic problem of complexity. The preacher must remain faithful to the Word of God, but the living Word of God is not totally identical with the written Word of God in the Scriptures. The limitations of the Scriptures have been described in discussing the whole question of ministry.

The historical and cultural limitations of the Scriptures are also quite apparent in the whole area of morality.[4] Many of the most difficult moral problems facing our society today are never mentioned or even envisioned in the Scriptures. The Scriptures offer very little concrete advice on the major issues facing society today. When one looks at the Scriptures in terms of their own times, there is a most interesting phenomenon. The Scriptures and the early Church really do not seem that preoccupied with questions of social morality. In fact, they seem to ignore the questions and even go along with the existence of abuses such as slavery. This has always been a difficult point for Christian apologists to explain. Some Christians have seen in the Scriptures, especially in the New Testament, a program for the

---

[4] For a discussion of this particular question, see Edouard Hamel, S.J., "L'Usage de l'Écriture Sainte en théologie morale," *Gregorianum*, XLVII (1966), 53-85; James M. Gustafson, "The Place of Scripture in Christian Ethics: A Methodological Study," *Interpretation*, XXIV (1970), 430-455. My essay on the subject, "The Role and Function of the Scriptures in Moral Theology," can be found in *Catholic Moral Theology in Dialogue* (Notre Dame, Indiana: Fides Publishers, 1972), pp. 24-64.

change and betterment of society.[5] Others maintain that there is no direct concern for creating a system of social ethics in the New Testament Scriptures.[6]

The problem of going from the Scriptures to the concrete situation of today's existence obviously remains an important question not only for the homilist but also for the moral theologian or Christian ethicist. The whole hermeneutic problem cannot be avoided. Paul Lehmann in his book on Christian ethics begins by pointing out the difference between biblical ethics and Christian ethics.[7] The Scriptures in themselves do not furnish adequate guidance for the moral issues facing our society today. There are sources of interpretation and, it seems, also knowledge outside the Scripture which help in discovering the Word of God for a particular situation. In a sense this realization merely complicates the problem for the preacher of the Word. This question has been answered in different ways by different theologies, and there is neither theoretical nor practical agreement among all Christians or even among Catholics on precisely how this should be done.

It lies outside the scope of this chapter to delve deeply into the different theological approaches to this question. The scope remains the narrower scope of ministering the moral Word of God to the Chris-

[5] Walter Rauschenbusch, *Christianity and the Social Crisis* (New York: Harper Torchbook, 1964). This was originally published by Macmillan in 1907.

[6] Rudolf Schnackenburg, *The Moral Teaching of the New Testament* (New York: Herder and Herder, 1965), p. 11.

[7] Paul L. Lehmann, *Ethics in a Christian Context* (New York: Harper and Row, 1963), pp. 26-32.

tian people in the various situations in which they and society find themselves. Again part of the crisis facing the preacher is evident. Obviously there will be theological presuppositions contained in whatever is said about this relationship between the Word of God in the Scriptures and the Word of God as related to the moral questions of contemporary existence.

In general my own theological prejudices will emerge in my frequent insistence on complexity. There are both methodological and substantive reasons for this working bias. From a methodological viewpoint problems arise in many different disciplines from the failure to consider all the elements which must go into the situation. This is also true in theology. Errors frequently arise from a failure to consider all the aspects which must enter into the situation. By forgetting one aspect, the whole process remains somewhat distorted. The danger of finite man is at times to close down and exclude elements which should enter into consideration. Yet one can also abuse this insistence on complexity. In the name of complexity one can refuse to act, or put off decisions. The crisis in culture mentioned earlier comes precisely from the need to judge, decide and act in the midst of complexity. One must learn to live with this tension and not try to do away with the tension either by disregarding the complexity and naively working on the assumption of a greater simplicity than in reality exists, or by just putting off all decisions and actions until a greater certitude can be obtained.

There are also substantive reasons behind the insistence on complexity. Roman Catholic theology in the better part of its theological tradition has emphasized this complexity especially in the area of coming to moral judgments and decisions. Catholic theology has rejected approaches associated with Scripture alone or faith alone or grace alone. The Catholic recognition of the need for human reasoning in determining what is moral and human opens up such a system to receive all kinds of knowledge and information about man. Thus theology in examining moral questions must be open to philosophy as well as to the data of the behavioral, social and physical sciences.[8]

The problem of complexity exists not only in trying to relate the Word of God in the Scriptures to the Word of God for contemporary problems, but also in trying to determine the teaching of the Scriptures on a particular point. In the scriptural revelation itself there tends to be some diversity. Often in homiletic or even scientific considerations those parts of the Scritpures which do not agree with preconceived notions receive little or no emphasis.

In an older climate in Catholic thinking primary emphasis was on law and the commandments rather than faith. Thus the most important personage in the Old Testament tended to be Moses and not

---

[8] For an illustration of this in Catholic moral theology, see Bernard Häring, C.SS.R., *The Law of Christ*, 3 vols. (Westminster, Md.: Newman Press, 1961, 1963, 1966).

Abraham.[9] Certain forms of more Orthodox Protestantism with their rightful emphasis on faith and salvation as God's saving gift to man in Jesus Christ neglected other aspects of the Scriptures which emphasize the place of man's response and his works.[10] The social gospel of liberal Protestantism, on the other hand, emphasized especially the prophets in the Old Testament and the Sermon on the Mount in the New Testament because these selections illustrated well the basic tenets of social gospel teaching. However, there was a neglect of other aspects of Scripture which stressed faith, sin and the redemption.[11] These illustrations taken mostly from theology suffice to show the dangers even in considerations of the written Word of God when only one particular aspect of the Word of God is considered. A polemical exclusion always remains a danger in our understanding and use of the Word of God both in theology and in preaching.

These pages have tried to situate the problems faced by the minister of the Word in relating the Word to the moral life of Christians today. His first responsibility is to the Word of God and not to another word. His second responsibility is to the whole Word of God and not just to a particular part of the Word of God. His third responsibility is to all God's

---

[9] Philippe Delhaye, *Le Décalogue et sa place dans la morale chrétienne* (Bruxelles: La Pensée Catholique, 1963). This and the following two references point up the dangers mentioned in the text.

[10] James Sellers, *Theological Ethics* (New York: Macmillan, 1966), pp. 39-53.

[11] John Dillenberger and Claude Welch, *Protestant Christianity* (New York: Charles Scribner's Sons, 1954), pp. 241-254.

people who want to be nourished by that Word. With this understanding of the problematic three important areas will be discussed which relate to the preaching of the moral Word of God—the moral and ethical aspects of the Word of God in relation to the whole Word of God, the eschatological aspects which again are a source of tension, and the precise question of the specificity of the preached Word concerning concrete human questions.

THE WHOLE WORD OF GOD

An important first problem area is the relationship of the moral aspect of the Word of God to the whole Word of God. Scholars frequently divide the New Testament writings into kerygma, didache and parenesis. The scriptural Word of God definitely contains a moral aspect, but the moral aspect does not appear as the primary characteristic. Thus the stage is set for the danger of overemphasizing the moral aspects of the Word of God at the expense of the whole Word of God. The minister of the Word can never forget his responsibility to preach the whole Word of God.

The Old Testament views the moral aspect of the Word in terms of man's response to the covenant gift of God. Even the so-called ten commandments, which in the original are called the ten words, form part of the response of man to the gift of the covenant.[12] One thus errs by seeing the Old Testa-

---

[12] Matthew J. O'Connell, "Commandment in the Old Testament," *Theological Studies*, XXI (1960), 351-403.

ment primarily in terms of law and commandments, for the saving Word of God in the Old Testament was the covenant election by which Yahweh promised that he would be their God, and they would be his people. The moral or ethical teaching of the Old Testament thus is a religious ethic, in the sense that man's moral response and actions must always be seen in relation to God and his loving gift. This is also true of the New Testament.[13]

The preacher cannot reduce the Word of God only to its moral aspects. The Word of God as preached in the Church also has other important limitations in the moral area. The Word of God and the Church are not the only or even the primary elements present in the attempts to bring about a more human and moral life for men existing in the world today. Earlier, mention was made of a new type of triumphalism which has crept into some Catholic theology and Catholic life. Some seem to think that the Word of God and the Church exist primarily as the leading agent of social change. The primary task of the Church does not consist in the changes to be wrought in society, although the Church will always have an interest in this precisely because of the relevance of the Word of God as lived and preached for all the situations of human existence. We cannot forget that there are many other individuals and groups with a competency and a responsibility to play a role in making and keeping human life more human. The Word of God and those who gather together to be nourished by

---

[13] Schnackenburg, pp. 13, 14.

the Word and Work of Jesus do have a role to play
in this area of bringing about the better society and
working here for the building up of the kingdom;
but this is not the primary function of the Church,
nor is the Church the only group working in this
particular area. One must resist the temptation to
make the Church the sole or the primary contribu-
tor to the moral renewal of society.

The primary aspect of the Word of God is not the
moral aspect, but rather the Word of God as gift.
The gospel itself is literally and really the good
news—the gift of God to us and our freedom and
salvation in the new life in Christ Jesus. The first responsibility of the minister of the Word is to proclaim this good news. To celebrate the gift of God
in Word and sacrament is the first function of the
Church. The preacher of the Word can never forget
this primary aspect of the Saving Word of God.
Those who constantly preach only about moral
issues and questions are not totally faithful to the
Word of God in its entirety. This gift aspect of the
Word calls forth praise and gratitude from all those
who have received this saving and efficacious Word.

The Word of God is not only gift, but it is also a
Word of promise and hope. Especially in the second
chapter this aspect of the Word of God was seen as
playing an important role in the spirituality of the
minister. He who ministers the Word and Work of
Jesus finds precisely in this Word the hope and the
promise that become the ultimate source of his joy
and commitment. The covenant promise of Yahweh
to his people was the source of their hope as they
struggled in their existence as the people of God.

There is an intimate connection between the Word
of God as gift and as promise. Precisely because of
the many gifts that God has given to us in the past,
we are not only grateful but also hopeful for the future. His Word is always a Word of promise and
hope. The promise lies at the heart of the Old Testament notion of the covenant and the spirituality of
the poor of Yahweh. The good news of the New
Testament remains always a promise to the hearer
of the Word. The resurrection of Jesus constitutes
the pledge and the promise of the fullness of the
resurrection which will one day belong to his faithful followers. Preaching the Word, celebrating the
Word must always emphasize this aspect of hope
and promise.

The Word of God is also challenge. In a sense the
challenge aspect of the Word of God can correspond roughly to the moral aspect of the Word of
God. The Word of God challenges us to act towards
others in the same way that he has acted towards
us. This challenge aspect of the Word of God forms
an integral part of the Word of God but is not its
whole meaning. The challenge of the Word of God
is all the more important because of our own sinfulness. We must be challenged to continually change
our hearts and rise above our selfishness and sinfulness.

Although one can view the challenge aspect of
the Word of God as roughly corresponding to the
moral aspect of the Word of God, one can also consider the moral aspect of the Word of God the response of man to the threefold aspects of the Word
of God. Man's response to the Word of God as gift,
promise and challenge can furnish the basic struc-

ture for understanding the moral life of the believer
in the light of the Word of God. The Word of God
itself obviously includes such a response. In moral
theology today there is a greater emphasis on the
centrality of response and responsibility. The primary model for understanding the moral life of man
should not be in terms of law or relationship to the
will of God, but rather in terms of man's response
to the loving gift of God.[14]

No matter how one sees the moral aspect of the
Word of God, all must agree that the moral aspect
is only one part of the total Word of God so that the
preacher of the Word does not fulfill his responsibilities to the whole Word of God if he limits himself only to moral questions. All the aspects of the
Word of God; that is, as gift, as promise, and as
challenge, must play a role in the preaching of the
Word of God if the preacher is faithful to his trust
to the whole Word of God.

The preacher constantly must criticize himself in
the light of the fullness of the Word of God. To
neglect any of these three elements distorts his function as a preacher of the Word. In the Scriptures or
the written Word of God one can find verified this
same threefold aspect of the Word. Thus in con-
structing homilies, the minister of the Word could
well imply this as a critical tool or even as a schema
for the development of his homily.

Take the beatitudes as an example. Scripture
scholars point out that the Scriptures were employed by the different biblical authors in the con-

---

[14] Albert R. Jonsen, *Responsibility in Modern Religious
Ethics* (Washington: Corpus Books, 1968).

text of the needs and the circumstances in which they found themselves. The beatitudes, at least in one theory of their scriptural development, well illustrate this threefold aspect of the Word of God.[15] In their original form the beatitudes were probably a messianic proclamation of the gifts that had been given to man. Happy are you because this gift of salvation has now been given to you. The proper response is naturally one of gratitude, praise and thanksgiving for the messianic gift. The beatitudes can also be understood in terms of a promise, and Luke has used the beatitudes precisely in this manner as is evident from his reaction of them. Luke realized that the messianic blessings proclaimed in the beatitudes had not yet been fully given, so Luke saw them as a promise of what would be given in the future. Luke contrasts the situation of man in this life with the future life as is evident from his introduction of the contrasting "now" and "then" into his use of the beatitudes. Happy are you who are hungry now and weep now, for then you will be satisfied and you will laugh.

Matthew's use of the beatitudes definitely has a moralizing (in the good sense of the term) or a cathechizing purpose. He uses the beatitudes to instill the attitudes and characteristics which describe the life of the follower of Jesus in this world. This is again evident from some changes and redactions made in his version of the beatitudes. The tendency to spiritualize the beatitudes; e.g., poor in spirit,

---

[15] Jacques Dupont, O.S.B., *Les Beatitudes* (Bruges: Éditions de l'Abbaye de Saint-André, 1954).

pure of heart, plus the frequent references to justice or righteousness, indicates that Matthew is employing the beatitudes to describe dispositions, attitudes and virtues which should mark the life of the follower of Jesus.

The threefold understanding of the Word of God can be applied to other biblical passages. Take, for example, the parable of the prodigal son which some Scripture scholars prefer to call the parable of the merciful father precisely because the story accentuates the mercy and forgiveness of the father. God's forgiveness is the great gift which men in no way earn or merit. The response of the grateful receiver of the gift must be one of praise and gratitude. Worship or praise to God for his gifts thus occupies an important place in the life of the Christian. The Word as promise reminds us that God is always ready to show mercy and forgive so that even in our darkest moments his promise remains the source of our hope. The Word as challenge can be seen in many different dimensions. There is the challenge to respond to the Father's gift and wholeheartedly return to the house of the Father. There is the challenge to act toward others in the same way the Father has acted toward us, and not to respond with the attitude of the elder son who could not fathom the real meaning of love and mercy.

The threefold nature of the Word of God stands out as the very nature of the Word of God in all its aspects and as a citerion for judging faithfulness to the Word of God in preaching. Obviously this does not mean that each homily will always contain these three aspects. For the sake of the congregation, at the very least, there should be different formats and outlines. But the whole preaching of the Word over a period of time must be faithful to this threefold aspect of the Word. To neglect the moral aspect of the Word or to make the moral aspect the exclusive characteristic of preaching would both constitute failures in the preacher's responsibility to the whole Word of God.

ESCHATOLOGICAL TENSIONS

A second important problem facing the minister entrusted to preach the Word of God to the Christian people has its theological roots in eschatology, but surfaces for the preacher of the Word in a number of different ways. The same basic problem is one of the tensions present in both Christian life and Christian ministry. The moral message of the Word of God includes the ideals of peace, love, community and reconciliation. Reconciliation in a very important theme both in terms of the meaning of the Word of God and in the context of the particular society in which we live. The message of Jesus Christ clearly calls for the reconciliation of all men —rich and poor, young and old; black, brown, red and white; male and female—in Christ Jesus. Our contemporary society knows great divisions and is in need of the healing power of God which can bring about this reconciliation. As individuals we experience the problems we have had with others and the bitterness which often remains. Meditating on the gospel passage, which tell us if we have anything against our brother, to leave our gift at the altar and first become reconciled with our brother, our consciences are uneasy and guilty.

Although the importance of reconciliation remains almost self-evident in the Christian context, yet there seems to be another side to the story. If the preacher speaks out on controversial moral or societal issues, he will probably create more division and tension among an already divided people. The same problematic in a more theoretical framework is the relationship between the prophetic aspect of the Word of God and the reconciling message of the Word. In many ways the prophets of the Old Testament were far from being agents of reconciliation for all the people. Part of the difficulty with the prophetic mission itself, as seen in the lives of the great prophets such as Jeremiah, was loneliness and isolation. The prophet was often a sign of contradiction and experienced personal anguish because of this. Jesus himself remains as the prophet par excellence who stirred up much opposition within the community even to the point of being crucified. The ministry for Paul was not one success after another but truly the experience of the paschal mystery.

The very challenging aspect of the Word of God means that at times it will be a two edged sword in the sense of bringing about some division within the community. The problem does become acute for the preacher of the Word who honestly strives to fulfill his responsibilities to the Word and to his people. How does one bring together the reconciling and the prophetic aspects of the Word of God? If reconciliation becomes the primary or the only object of Christian preaching, perhaps an aspect of the Chris-

tian message is being overlooked. Despite the great
emphasis in the Word of God on peace, unity and
love, there are still times that call for the prophetic
voice that will introduce discord and division. Many
times these are only situations of a false and psuedo-
peace which definitely need to be unmasked. As
long as we are living in this imperfect world, the
Word of God will always have an accusing function.

From a theological perspective the imperfections
and sinfulness of our existing humanity are the reasons for the fact that at times the Word of God to
us is an accusing word. None of us has fully
achieved the reality of the new life in Christ Jesus,
but we constantly fall short. The fullness of the
gospel message with its emphasis on the love and
service of our neighbor always has an accusing aspect for us who live in this situation before the fullness of the resurrection. Reconciliation is only one
aspect of the Christian message which will never be
totally realized until the end of time.

To a certain extent there is also a danger of overemphasizing the reality of love and the reality of
peace which are two very important characteristics
of the Word of God. Woe to the minister of the
Word if he fails to constantly challenge his hearers
to live more in accord with these ideals. But the
realization that we live in a somewhat sinful world
this side of the fullness of the eschaton calls for a
realistic assessment of human existence. Love and
peace are very important realities in the Christian
message, but they can become romanticized and
sentimentalized. Likewise at times one cannot speak
to the situation in a relevant way if one only talks

in terms of love or peace. Labor disagreements are not susceptible to a solution in the more simplistic terms of love and peace. The idealism and driving force of love and peace must be kept, but tempered by a realistic understanding of the times in which we live.

Peace is the great messianic gift to us, but in a sense there will never be the totality and fullness of peace in this world. Peace in its fullness is God's gift at the end time. The Christian can never be satisfied with the lack of peace but must always struggle in his attempt to bring about a greater sharing of peace. There is a danger of being overly romantic about the gospel message of peace. Very often, just as in the matter of unity, the peace which is existing is a false peace and must be shattered. Likewise one must realize that in the pilgrim existence of the present, one must realistically be prepared to deal with situations in which peace does not exist.

To a certain extent the same tension even exists in the matter of love. Obviously this is the ideal toward which Christians must strive. In this present existence love is not the only factor present. At times there are and always will be struggles for power. Christian theology has at times recognized the need for the use of power, force and even violence in such areas as strikes in labor disputes, the need for a police force to protect individuals and the community, the possibility of just war and even the possibility of revolution and tyrannicide. In all these areas there remains the twofold danger of either demanding nothing but the fullness of love or else too easily accepting the status quo with its imperfections and its use of power, force and even violence for merely selfish purposes.

A Christian can never deny the importance of love, peace and reconciliation, but again there are circumstances where power, force and violence might be necessary. One must in these areas admit the existence of complexity without merely saying yes to existing structures which in themselves are so imperfect. In our day and age the danger also exits of romanticizing force and violence as has so often been done in the last few years. I can never deny the fact that at times force and even violence will be necessary, but the Christian realist understands the problems and difficulties that can so easily ensue.

A perennial temptation in all these areas is to harness the absoluteness of the Christian message behind a certain idea or concept or way of proceeding. Some people will too easily baptize the existing social structures and identify them with the will of God and his plan for men. Others will say that revolution is the only way to bring about liberation for all men, and this is what God is doing in the world today to make and keep human life more human. At the very least one has to be aware of the existence of this problem.

In many ways the root problem in all these questions touches on the matter of eschatology. The ethical teaching of Jesus as found in the synoptic gospels has always created a problem for Christian theologians and preachers. There is a magnificent simplicity about this ethic (do not worry about what you eat or drink; unless you hate your father and mother; if your brother strikes you on the cheek, turn to him the other cheek as well) and a gnawing realization that in this world problems tend to be more complex with many factors entering into the considerations. This just illustrates in a graphic way the questions raised by theoretical teaching of Jesus. Many different solutions have been proposed for coming to grips with and explaining the ethical teaching of Jesus, but most of these solutions recognize the need for some eschatological presuppositions.[16]

In general, my solution to the practical questions mentioned as facing the preacher of the Word and the questions raised by the very ethical teaching of Jesus adopts a concept of eschatology in the process of realization.[17] We live in between the two comings of Jesus; we have received the newness of life and participate in the life of the resurrection through baptism yet we wait and yearn for the fullness of His final coming. The second coming of Jesus will bring to completion and perfection the work of redemption. As pilgrim Christians we are going forward toward that second coming, but realizing that our efforts will always fall short, since the completion of redemption remains God's gra-

---

[16] Richard H. Hiers, *Jesus and Ethics* (Philadelphia: Westminster Press, 1968).

[17] For my development of the solution to the question of the ethical teaching of Jesus, see my essay, "The Relevancy of the Ethical Teaching of Jesus," in *A New Look at Christian Morality* (Notre Dame, Indiana: Fides Publishers, 1968), pp. 1-23.

cious gift to us. There is both continuity and discontinuity between the present and the future.[18]

The danger of collapsing this tension exists in two
opposite ways. On the one hand, some think that the
fullness of the eschaton is already present and fail
to consider the human imperfections and sinfulness
which are and always will in some degree continue
to exist in this world. As mentioned in Chapter Two
there were many in the last decade who suffered
from the theological disease of a chronically collapsed eschaton. Such a vision was naively utopian
in its hopes for human and social progress and unfortunately forgot the more brutal characteristics
of human existence.

On the other hand, the tension is also collapsed
by those who fail to see the pull of the future as a
negative critique on all existing structures and institutions. One can never be content with the situation
of the present because in the Christian viewpoint
or horizon the present situation also reflects some
of man's imperfections and some of his sinfulness.
Love, peace and reconciliation will never be fully
present until the culmination of God's saving gift
occurs in the fullness of the kingdom. Although
realizing the imperfections of the present, Christians have an obligation to strive to overcome these
limitations and work for a greater participation in
the peace, unity and love of the reign of God.

There is a tendency on the part of all of us to lose

---

[18] These same eschatological presuppositions underlie my
criticism in the last chapter of paradox as the primary model for
understanding the way in which God works in this world.

sight of our own limitations and the limitations of man in our human existence. Our own limitations are obvious in our ability to so easily forget the plight and circumstances of those who are less fortunate. The impulse of Christianity with its universality and its tendency to extend our horizon and vision to the utmost argues against such a narrowness of vision. The Christian must always try to improve the present situation, but improvement and change involve a long struggle and call for a commitment which does not find its ultimate motive in the success of its ventures.

Today those who realize the imperfections of the present and the great limitations of the status quo often fail to understand the long struggle involved in the need to bring about change. There is much talk, and rightly so, about freedom and liberation today. People are rightly trying to involve themselves in the movements that call for liberation and work to bring it about. However, a glance at history reminds us of how slow the process has been in the area of freedom and liberation.

Man has known many types of enslavement in the past, and as he breaks through in freedom he comes to know other enslavements. There is thus the need for constant vigilance. In many ways primitive man was imprisoned by nature and the cruel forces of nature which took their toll in privation, disease and death. Man has gradually been freed from the powers of brute nature, but he has not escaped other forms of imprisonment. Technology and the machine in their own way have captured and enslaved man, as many people are only too willing to admit. Political freedom has been obtained for many people after long struggles, but there remain many other types of imprisonment such as economic enslavement.

Perhaps a new form of slavery for some is in the area of psychological freedom. Man's struggle against the forces that enslave him will not end, for there are so many barriers to the true freedom of man. Sometimes his desire for a wrong kind of freedom is itself the greatest form of slavery. We brag about the freedom of our own society. Our youth seem to exemplify it in all they do. But take another look. To dress in jeans has become as rigid a code as the old shirt and tie. The "in" people must wear big buckles and have medallions. There is some irony in these observations, but the point is that even where we naively think that freedom has been obtained there remain so many areas of enslavement. This is a point that cannot be forgotten. The struggle in all these areas is never over. The imperfections and even the sinfulness of our pilgrim existence will always be part and parcel of our human existence.

Those who expect changes to come about quickly and easily do not appreciate the very nature of our existence as is well illustrated in history. The problem with some reform movements in society and in the Church today is precisely in this area. It is easy to see the sinfulness and imperfections in others but not always in ourselves. But the Scripture reminds Christians about the beam in our own eye. The Christian vision or horizon with its eschatological presuppositions realizes the imperfections and sinfulness that beset not only the present structures but also the evolutionary or revolutionary movements which try to change this structure. This again does not mean that all things are equally engulfed with imperfection and sinfulness so that nothing can be done. By no means. The Christian imperative always calls for growth, change and development in the existing person or structure, but it realizes that such changes do not come about easily. At the same time this pilgrim existence also characterizes the movements for changes which must always be on guard against the charge of hypocrisy and the failure to see and admit their own shortcomings.

An understanding of eschatology in the process of realization but never fully present until God's gift becomes complete at the end of time will furnish the preacher of the Word of God with an horizon or perspective with which he can better understand the reality of the times in which we live. In a sense this perspective of eschatology in the process of realization but which will always fall far short of God's final gift corresponds roughly with the threefold aspect of the Word of God as already developed. The Word of God is gift and challenge but also promise. The fullness is in the form of promise which means that God will bring to conclusion the work he has begun. But as challenge the Word of God also entails a struggle on our part to transcend the present and work for its change and betterment with the realization that our efforts are absolutely necessary but in no way sufficient, since the kingdom remains God's gift to us in its eschatological fullness. This perspective should help the preacher of the Word, but it still calls for great insight in judging in particular situations.

THE PROBLEM OF SPECIFICITY

A third area of concern in the crisis of preaching the moral Word of God concerns the specificity of the Word of God as addressed to very particular and complex problems facing man today. One can briefly summarize the dilemma raised in the introductory pages of this chapter. On the one hand, the Word of God should have some relevance and meaning for man in the situations in which he finds himself; but on the other hand, the scriptural word is inadequate in dealing with the complex problems of our changed existence so that the preacher of the Word needs some other guidance in addition to the Scripture and a great expertise because of the complexity of such problems. But, if he then talks about these questions, is he really preaching the Word of God or his own word? The problem of how specific the preacher of the Word should be focuses on this dilemma.

This chapter has already established the fact that there is a moral aspect to the Word of God but has cautioned that this is not the only aspect of the Word of God. The problem does not concern only the problem of relating the Word of God to the very specific questions of contemporary life. There is even some problem in systematizing the moral teaching of the Scriptures. There has been no agreement within Christian Churches or even within the Roman Catholic Church on the exact synthesis and systematization of the moral teaching of Jesus or the

Scriptures. In a sense the preacher of the Word does not have to operate at the same level of reflective systematization as the theologian, but he should at least be aware of the problems.

The most obvious summary of the moral teaching of Jesus would seem to be the commandment of love of God and neighbor.[19] Love obviously is important. But questions immediately arise. Is it the same kind of love we have toward God and our neighbor? Is it related in any way or opposed to the love of self? What are the elements which enter into this love? Others have not chosen love as the best synthetic understanding of the moral teaching of Jesus. Conversion occupies a central place in the Scriptures as is evident at least in Mark's summary of the moral teaching of Jesus. Some theologians have seen conversion as central to the moral life of the Christian.[20] Ceslaus Spicq sees the moral teaching of Paul the Apostle in terms of a Trinitarian morality based on our relationship to the various persons in the Trinity.[21] Fritz Tillmann has developed his understanding in terms of the following

---

[19] This position has been advocated by many in the tradition of liberal Protestantism. See James M. Gustafson, "Christian Ethics," in *Religion,* ed. Paul Ramsey (Englewood Cliffs: Prentice-Hall, 1965), pp. 309-316.

[20] Bernard Häring, C.SS.R., "Conversion," in P. Delhaye *et al., Pastoral Treatment of Sin* (New York: Desclee, 1968) pp. 87-176.

[21] Ceslaus Spicq, O.P., *The Trinity in Our Moral Life According to Saint Paul* (Westminster, Md.: Newman Press, 1963). But Spicq has also stressed the importance of *agape* in his *Agape in the New Testament,* 3 vols. (St. Louis: B. Herder, 1963, 1965, 1966). In his treatment of New Testament morality as such Spicq does not attempt a synthesis: *Théologie Morale du Nouveau Testament,* 2 vols. (Paris: Gabalda, 1965).

of Jesus.[22] These examples illustrate the diversity existing on the somewhat simpler question of the systematization of the ethical teaching of Jesus.

I would tend to agree with the position of H. Richard Niebuhr that neither love nor any other virtue or attitude can become a total synthesis for the ethical teaching of Jesus.[23] These various opinions have been brought up to show that problems exist even in trying to systematize and synthesize the moral teaching of Jesus. However, the preacher of the moral Word of Jesus does not necessarily have to attempt such a rigorous systematization.

All should agree that the moral aspect of preaching the Word of God should not be primarily concerned with very complex and concrete questions. This does not arise only from the difficulty of relating the Word of God to these situations, but also from the preachers obligation to all God's people. The people to whom he is entrusted to preach the Word of God find themselves in many diverse circumstances. It would be impossible from both practical and theological viewpoints to consider all these different situations. Thus it is obvious that the preacher of the Word cannot frequently descend into the particulars of a complex situation.

Generally speaking, the preacher of the Word must talk about the attitudes and dispositions which the Christain message proposes for the followers of

[22] Fritz Tillmann, *The Master Calls* (Baltimore: Helicon, 1960).

[23] H. Richard Niebuhr, *Christ and Culture* (New York: Harper Torchbook, 1956), pp. 11-29.

Jesus. Even though the preacher like the theologian cannot find an adequate synthesis or systematization of the Christian ethical teaching, nonetheless preaching the Word of God calls for an emphasis on those moral themes that so often do appear in the Scriptures. The great themes of gratitude, thanksgiving, love, hope, and a willingness to sacrifice self for others must form an integral part of the moral aspect of the Word of God. On this level there certainly is and should be a general acceptance of the important themes in such moral teaching.

The problem becomes much more acute as one descends from the general to the more specific. How specific should the preacher of the Word become? The Word of God should have some meaning for the whole life of man if we truly believe in God as the Lord of history. The Word of God cannot be foreign to any human situation. Somehow or other it would seem that the Word of God has something to say on complex problems such as welfare laws, open housing, the war in Southeast Asia and the ecological problem. But what precisely can and should the preacher of the Word say on these and similar issues?

Yet, the contemporary preacher of the Word also recognizes the complexity of modern life and the manifold aspects of any one particular problem. The solution of problems calls for expertise and competencies which the preacher of the Word does not necessarily have. Likewise they often call for a knowledge of the facts and the data which he might not always possess. Human prudential judgments will frequently be made in the realization that amidst such complexity it remains difficult to determine the solution to the problem.

The temptation to an overly simplistic solution has often existed for the Christian preacher because of some of the eschatologically conditioned statements of the ethical teaching of Jesus. But one might not always be able to solve human problems in this world by walking the extra mile or turning the other cheek. One, especially a preacher with the trust to preach the Word of God to the people of God, must proceed with caution in these same areas and at the same time he must be courageous enough to raise his voice even when this is unpopular.

Mention has already been made of a new form of triumphalism in the Catholic Church and also in other Christian Churches which expects the Church and ministers of the Word of God to supply answers to the problems facing contemporary society and to be the leader in the struggle for a renewed society in which the rights of all men are protected. But the Church is not the only or the major instrument working for the reform of society. This is not the principal task of the Church, yet the Church and the gospel definitely must have something to say in this area. The triumphalism comes in expanding the role and function of the Church while at the same time not giving enough importance to the other factors and institutions which must be working in these areas.

Even here there is a difference between the role of the Church and the relevancy of the Word of God in these areas. Individual Christians very often operate in these areas not precisely as Church but in other capacities such as politicians, statesmen, lawyers, community organizers. In a sense the Church today cannot and should not be all things to all men. The very complexity of our existence argues strongly against this approach. Within the Church we must recognize a diversity of roles and functions. One cannot simplistically reduce all the roles to the same thing. There are different roles and functions for individual members of the Church, especially in terms of the numerous other societies, institutions and communities to which they belong, for the smaller sub-communities within the Church, and for the Church itself.

This triumphalism frequently goes hand in hand with a presumed great certitude on very complex questions. At times the prophetic voice does become harsh, shrill and apparently very certain. The prophetic voice will always be required in the life of the Church, and the Christian who is truly open should never forget the need for the prophetic voice. However, on complex, societal problems I do not think that one can usually achieve such a degree of certitude.

There is also, from my viewpoint, a poor theology of the Word of God that tends to see a greater certitude in these specific areas than I think is usually possible. This theological tendency can best be described as a theological actualism, which sees God in terms of his actions in this world. Such a theology has generally been associated with an aversion to a metaphysical understanding of Christian ethics. The basic theology stems from the belief that God as the Lord of history is acting in our world. The Christian preceives what God is doing and then responds to this. Such a theology is associated with the name of Paul Lehmann.[24]

Basically I have two major difficulties with this approach. First of all, few if any criteria are given for discerning precisely what God is doing in the world. How do we "lock in" to what the action of God is? In these complex questions it appears that we need some kind of criteria as guidelines for discovering what the concrete action of God is. This complaint has been frequently brought up against such an approach.[25] The second objection is somewhat related. One can, and as a Christian should, have great certainty that God is working in this world, but in the midst of complexity this certitude on particular, specific questions is not what it is on the more general attitudes or dispositions such as love, freedom, hope and humility. As one descends from the general to the specific there is bound to be a lesser possibility of certitude and the admission of a greater plurality of possible options and opinions. Often it is difficult to say precisely what God is doing. The theology that thinks of God as acting sees each act in itself and presumes that man can know what God is doing with some certitude. This particular theology when carried to an extreme seems to claim with too much certitude what should be done in complex cases.

---

[24] Lehmann, *Ethics in a Christian Context*.
[25] James M. Gustafson, "Love Monism," in John C. Bennett, *et al., Storm Over Ethics* (No place given: United Church Press, 1967), pp. 26-37.

I would employ a more organic and somewhat more structured understanding of how God does act in the world and how man should respond. One can have more certitude about the generic dispositions required of the Christian than he can have about specific questions. There are more universal guidelines which help us to discern what God is doing. I would not necessarily accept the metaphysical underpinnings of Thomist theology or the Catholic natural law theory of the past, but likewise I cannot accept the seemingly wide open approach of some today. By the very fact of specificity and complexity, one must admit a greater degree of incertitude about how the Christian should respond and at the same time the fact that there might be a number of possible approaches for the Christian.

In Roman Catholic theology at the present time, this very aspect of complexity argues for the fact that within the pale of the Roman Catholic faith commitment there can be and is theological pluralism in the sense that there is no longer such a thing as the perennial philosophy, but there are many different philosophies and many different theological methodologies. Likewise on very complex issues it will be difficult to speak about *the* Catholic position on a certain question because of the complexity of the question and the many judgments which enter into the picture before the final judgment is made.[26] One then must logically see the effects of this complexity right across the board.

---

[26] For an illustration of this in the question of abortion, see *Theological Studies,* XXXI (March 1970).

AN OPPOSING POSITION

An opposite stand is taken by those who say the preacher of the Word should not discuss or mention social issues, since these are outside the purview of the Word of God. There has been a form of fundamentalism which has never concerned itself with social issues and which thus reserves the Word of God for other matters. Religion should not enter into the sphere of politics is the way in which this is very often expressed. However, here again one shrinks the meaning of the Word of God and reduces it to only one part of our human existence. I cannot accept such a narrow role for the Word of God.

The complexity argument has been employed by others in such a way as to say that the Church and to a certain extent the preacher of the Word should not be involved in specific, complex social questions. Paul Ramsey has condemned the practice of the 1966 Conference on Church and Society sponsored by the World Council of Churches for the particularity of its judgments on moral issues.[27] Ramsey believes pronouncements on specific issues such as the War in Viet Nam lie beyond the competency of the Church as such. He summarizes the heart of his position: "The question is whether and how far such judgments may be deduced or adduced—or in any other way entailed—by the shared affirmations of *Christian* social ethics *as such*."[28] Thus in the midst

---

[27] Paul Ramsey, *Who Speaks for the Church?* (Nashville: Abingdon Press. 1967).

[28] *Ibid.*, p. 18.

of complexity Ramsey believes that the ultimate
judgment rests not on anything distinctively Christian as such but on one's political or economic
theory. Here people with the same Christian convictions and attitudes may and do disagree not precisely on Christian grounds but rather because of
different opinions on political strategy or economic
policy.

Ramsey's position ultimately rests on a distinction
"between Christian moral judgments on the one
hand and particular political, legal and military
judgments on the other; or between what is morally
permitted or prohibited and what is tactically or
prudentially advisable and practicable."[29] Earlier
he insisted that the specific solution of particular
problems depends on political prudence and
worldly wisdom. In these areas there can be legitimate diversity among Christians.[30] Ramsey comes
back again to this basic point, but phrases it somewhat differently. "It is high time for it to be acknowledged on all sides that not every decision is
a moral decision, and that not every moral decision
is a Christian decision. The bearing of God's will
and governance in relation to every aspect of human
life cannot possibly be construed in such a fashion
that supposes that there is a Christian shape or style
to every decision."[31]

I have two major difficulties with Ramsey's reasoning. First, his understanding of Christian. In the

[29] *Ibid.*, p. 53.
[30] *Ibid.*, p. 19.
[31] *Ibid.*, pp. 135, 136 ·

Catholic tradition human reason and the natural have a part to play in the Christian so that they cannot be ruled out as non-Christian, even though the Christocentric aspect has not always been evident. Theologizing within this background, I would claim that whatever is human is to that extent connected with the Christian and Christian. Catholics have always been willing to propose stands on moral issues which did not depend on anything exclusively Christian but which rested on the natural law which was common to all men. Thus I cannot accept this dichotomy between the Christian and the human.

The second problem concerns the dichotomy between the human or the Christian and the political, legal or military. I believe that except in relatively well understood issues the questions to which Ramsey refers are not just military or political or legal questions but are truly human questions. We have reacted, and rightly I believe, to the tendency in our society to have specialists in charge of everything. Military men should not run the Pentagon. School boards should include more than educators. There is always the need for the broad, human perspective which the specialist qua specialist cannot supply. Military, political and scientific knowledge must be in the service of man and not vice-versa. Any one science only sees a small part of the total human perspectives. The human can never be identified with the findings of any one science be it psychology, sociology, biology or political science.

The truly human judgment involves more than the data of any one science. This data is extremely helpful and necessary, but the human judgment must judge this in the light of many other considerations. The judgment that two plus two equals four is only a mathematical judgment and not a truly human judgment. But the judgment to devalue currency is a truly human judgment and involves more than the science of economics. Knowledge of economics is extremely important but cannot be the only consideration. Both practically and theoretically the human judgment cannot be equated with the judgment of a particular science or a particular discipline. Even though the judgment requires great economic or legal data, the judgment is ultimately a human judgment and involves more than just this one science. Truly human judgments which effect man and his society are more than merely economic or political or psychological judgments. They are human judgments.

A PROPOSED SOLUTION

Having rejected these other proposed solutions, my own solution should be somewhat evident. I believe that these questions affecting man and society are truly human judgments and that the Word of God has something to say about them. However in the midst of such complexity precisely because so many different factors enter into the specific judgment no one can claim in such a case that his response is *the only* Christian response to the question. The truth in Ramsey's argumentation is the fact that one cannot say that a person who holds a contrary position no longer is a good Christian.[32] In very specific matters precisely because of the complexity one can and should maintain that he can arrive at a Christian position but not *the* Christian position in the sense of excluding all others. There remains here the room for legitimate differences among Christians, however one can and should maintain the rightness of his own position and be able to say it is a Christian position. Since so many elements go into a situation, no one can claim absolute certitude for himself and his judgment. However, the preacher of the Word definitely has a right to propose and to hold his opinion as the one he thinks and judges to be right. But because of the complex nature of such judgments he cannot exclude someone else from the pale of Christianity precisely because he comes to a different conclusion.

The Word of God does have something to say to men in all the truly human decisions of their lives. In specific decisions this input might be comparatively small but it is still there. Likewise my theological understanding of the Word of God would enable it to include everything human, so that the judgment would not have to be based on something distinctively Christian or something found only in the Scriptures. There are many factors that must enter into such specific judgments, and they often

---

[32] Note that Ramsey is talking about statements of the Church on these issues and not statements of the preacher of the Word. One might argue for a legitimate difference between the two. I disagree, however, with the basic reasons proposed by Ramsey.

demand great study and expertise. However, the ultimate judgment is a truly human judgment.

Obviously the minister of the Word should not speak out on every complex issue facing our society. However his own Christian discernment should lead him to understand the gravity of some problems and the need to propose his understanding of the Word of God in these cases. As a preacher of the Word he must propose his judgment in such a way that he does not fail in his responsibilities to all the Christian people who want to be nourished by God's Word. This means that his preaching must include all the other aspects of the Word of God and not merely talk about social questions. Likewise, he must indicate how all Christians must take into account the various Christian attitudes, ideals and principles that should bear on the subject. Then he can show how he personally would understand these attitudes in this situation with all the data necessary to make proper judgments. But he must be careful not to forget that other Christians might come to different conclusions on issues. By proposing his solution he also stimulates people to reflect on their own conclusions and judgments.

What I have proposed here seems to be in continuity with the best of Roman Catholic theology. The competency of the magisterium to teach on moral matters has been admitted. However the hierarchical magisterium has most frequently done this in the area of natural law and has not claimed that there had to be a distinctively Christian aspect to the teaching. Interestingly enough, there has never been an infallible teaching on a moral matter. In theology a few years ago some proposed that the Church cannot teach infallibly on a matter which is only of the natural law. However, this does not go to the heart of the problem. The very complexity of specific moral problems is such that there cannot be an infallible teaching in this area.[33] Thus, teaching on specific moral matters belongs to the area of what has lately been called the authentic or authoritative, noninfallible, magisterial teaching. Recently Catholics have become more aware of the possibilities for a Catholic to dissent from such teaching and still be a loyal Roman Catholic.[34] This possibility of dissent will, in the future, be seen in more and more areas as is already evident in the area of abortion precisely because of the complexity of judging about the beginning of human life and the way in which conflict situations involving the fetus and other human lives or values should be determined.[35] In a sense in the future it will be impossible to speak about the Roman Catholic position on a particular, complex moral issue.

Notice the insistence on referring to specific, complex moral problems. Obviously, in keeping with my theological presuppositions one can have greater certitude and perhaps even speak about *the* Catholic or *the* Christian teaching when one speaks more generally and does not descend to specific, complex

---

[33] Daniel C. Maguire, "Moral Absolutes and the Magisterium," in *Absolutes in Moral Theology?*, ed. Charles E. Curran (Washington: Corpus Books, 1968).

[34] Charles E. Curran, Robert E. Hunt, et al., *Dissent In and For the Church* (New York: Sheed and Ward, 1969).

[35] See note 26.

problems. Thus, for example, one can say that opposition to discrimination because of race, creed or
color is the Christian position. But there could be
some doubt about what one means by discrimination. It is important to understand that in my argument the question hinges on the epistemological
understanding that as one descends to specifics
and particulars there will be great room for
disagreement.

Although the preacher of the Word should at
times discuss complex, societal issues and indicate
his Christian position, there are other ways in which
the preacher can fulfill his responsibilities in this regard. Very often these questions can be used as illustrations. Or he can ask his people to reflect on
why, for example, they oppose welfare reform to
make sure that discrimination or lack of charity or
personal or national selfishness are not the real
motives. Without proposing any particular solution,
the preacher can challenge his people to make sure
that un-Christian reasons have not entered into
their final judgment.

There is one Christian value or understanding of
a generic nature which has great importance in the
area of social morality but is too often lacking in
Christian consciousness and in preaching the Word
of God. This is the Christian prejudice or bias in
favor of the poor, the outcast and the downtrodden.
Paradoxically, the "objective Christian vision" includes this bias.

The gospel message itself underlines the privi-
leged position of the poor and the sinners in the
reign of God. Love of neighbor is seen especially in

terms of the love of the neighbor in need. The neighbor in need places a special claim upon the love and concern of the Christian. The Christian teaching on sin and selfishness reminds us of the narrowness of our perspective, which too easily seeks our own personal concerns. The preacher of the Word of God needs to challenge his hearers to approach problems of social morality with the Christian bias and prejudice. Such an outlook will often bring about surprisingly different practical conclusions and actions.

The preacher of the Word of God must remember, however, that the discussion of complex, moral issues is only a fraction and a comparatively small part of his total function of preaching the Word of God. The Word of God must be preached as gift, promise, and challenge. The moral aspect of this preaching is merely one aspect, and within the moral aspect primacy must be given to those general dispositions, ideals and principles which Christians should themselves incorporate in their own lives.

These theological reflections indicate the way in which the preacher of the Word can and should carry out his responsibilities. He must constantly question himself about the trust that has been committed to him—to preach the Word of God and the whole of God's Word to all God's people.